CINCINNATI GOETTA

CINCINNATI GOETTA

A Delectable History

DANN WOELLERT

AMERICAN PALATE

Published by American Palate
A Division of The History Press
Charleston, SC
www.historypress.com

Front cover, top: author's collection; *bottom*: courtesy of Mark Balasa, Queen City Sausage.
Back cover, left: courtesy of Mark Balasa, Queen City Sausage; *right*: author's collection.

First published 2019

Manufactured in the United States

ISBN 9781467142083

Library of Congress Control Number: 2019937037

Notice: The information in this book is true and complete to the best of our knowledge. It is offered without guarantee on the part of the author or The History Press. The author and The History Press disclaim all liability in connection with the use of this book.

To Owen, Jackson and Aidan, the next generation of goetta eaters and makers.

CONTENTS

Introduction

THE BIG GOETTA PROJECT

Cincinnati has a love affair with goetta. It's no secret. The top ten commerical producers of goetta in greater Cincinnati make an estimated two and a quarter million pounds of it annually. A true Cincinnatian has one or more of the following cooking utensils: a wort paddle to make beer, an oval plate to serve Cincinnati chili or a giant wooden paddle to stir goetta. After the question "Vas you efer in Zinzinnati," the second question is, "Hast du ever tasted Zinzinnati goetta?" It's truly amazing that an obscure winter peasant breakfast food has made it front and center of our regional pop culture.

Mention goetta anywhere outside of a fifty-mile radius of Cincinnati, and you'll get funny looks. But ask anyone inside that loop, and you'll get a TED Talk on whose is best, how best to prepare it and what condiments should be used to dress it. For those in greater Cincinnati, goetta is a lifestyle. It's the topic of tall tales and legends. There are T-shirts with goetta sayings and two Goettafests a year. But you can find goetta year-round. Locals know at least one of more than one hundred restaurants that serve goetta in its purest form or concocted into an innovative fusion dish. Most have a favorite local butcher, if they're not satisfied with the several commercial brands available at Kroger and big-box retailers. Although most like it fried crispy, the crispy vs. mushy debate has sparked family civil wars across the region. And don't even get started with what to dress it with. That conversation could last for hours.

The hardest thing is describing goetta to outsiders. My oldest friend from grade-school days, Mike, who prefers to dress his goetta with Frank's hot sauce, describes the origin of goetta as if Scottish haggis and a German sausage got together and produced a really tasty baby. His family comes from at least a four-generation goetta-eating family. I've heard others describe it as scrapple's tastier cousin. I like that description a lot. In food writing, goetta is always the Jan Brady to scrapple's Marcia. Goetta hasn't reached national status, yet. Online Scrabble doesn't recognize *goetta* as a word. And my iPhone is constantly autocorrecting my texts using *goetta*. Alexa responds that she doesn't know what goetta is made of. But then again, she was made in China. Siri does know about goetta, so that's encouraging.

I have relatives who no longer live in Cincinnati who say that whenever someone mentions goetta in a conversation, it's like finding a long-lost relative that they even know that goetta exists. This is also the branch of my family who boasts that they've never eaten commercially produced goetta, only homemade.

Long before there was Cincinnati chili, cheese coneys and Graeter's raspberry chip ice cream, there was goetta. Immigrants from northwestern Germany brought the legacy with them over a century ago to remind them of home. Only in the last fifty years has it been more than an obscure cold-weather breakfast food. It's reached the tipping point of cultural hipness.

Since 2013, the Cincinnati Food and Wine Classic has sponsored an event called Goetta Superstar. It positions three groups of chefs against one another in a live version of *Chopped*. The teams must use goetta and another secret ingredient to make a cohesive dish. One year, it was goetta and paw paws.

Goetta is mentioned in a song by local bluegrass band Jake Speed & the Freddies, "Queen City Christmas": "Queen City Eggnog tastes much betta', when you add a pound of goetta."

Andrew Zimmern tasted goetta at the Six Acres Bed and Breakfast in College Hill in a recent episode of *Bizarre Foods*. Episode seven of season twelve, titled "The Underground Railroad," connected goetta to the many Cincinnati Germans involved in the Underground Railroad and the abolitionist movement. It may have been fed locally to fugitive slaves, like the Cincinnati 28, a group that journeyed through the creek bed behind the B&B. Six Acres was built in the 1850s by Zebulon Strong, a Quaker abolitionist who helped escaping slaves.

The interesting thing about connecting goetta and fugitive slaves is that goetta is a lot like slave cooking. Goetta is based on taking lesser-quality cuts of meat and extending them with a grain. And that's exactly what slaves would do in their cooking. They were given the discarded cuts of meat from the wealthy masters and extend them with cooked greens or with a variety of beans. In Germany, the field workers, or *heurling*, on the large manors of German nobility were given the offcuts of meat from the owners of the manor and created the multitude of grain sausages or *gruetzwurst*, that birthed our goetta. How interesting would it be to find documentation that these slaves who escaped through Cincinnati had been fed goetta by German immigrant abolititionists, saw the similarity to their cooking and used goetta in their diets in the free communities where they settled in Canada?

Christmas is the busiest season for goetta. Most butchers and commercial producers say they make twice their normal amount during the winter holidays. Serving food is how we show people we love them. And for greater Cincinnatians, serving homemade or even store-bought goetta for breakfast over the holidays to our visiting relatives is the epitome of familial love. In fact, if visiting relatives aren't served goetta at a family holiday brunch, they might ask, "Does my family not love me anymore?!"

Celebrities and public figures have chimed in about goetta. It had reached such national exposure that President George W. Bush asked in 2006, "What is goetta?"

In a 1979 interview with Bill Moyers, Ronald Reagan said this: "We lived in a small town (Dixon, Illinois). It was from payday to payday with us, and I can remember one dish that I thought was delicious and it was only later that I realized why we had it. Have you ever heard of oatmeal meat? Well, you make oatmeal and you mix ground meat with it. Then you make a gravy just out of that, and then you serve that in a big pancake-like thing. Well, that was because we couldn't afford to have that pancake made of all meat." What President Reagan was referring to was hafer grits, or gritzwurst, a cousin to goetta that was common in the rural German immigrant communities of the Midwest.

When Drew Lachey, winner of *Dancing with the Stars* and 98 Degrees boyband heartthrob, was asked how he ate when training for the show, he said, "There's this stuff called goetta that's huge in Cincinnati. It's a German meat product—pork mixed with oats—that goes back a long way. I like to fry up some goetta and have breakfast for dinner." Then, when Drew and his brother Nick Lachey operated Lachey's Bar and Grille from 2015 to 2018, they had a Hair of the Dog Burger, with goetta, white cheese and a fried egg.

When I started out on the big goetta project, I had the intent of finding that original goetta recipe, the holy grail, the one that would prove where exactly in Germany our beloved goetta had originated. Goetta runs deep in my blood on both sides of my Germanic family. So I wanted to crack the geneaological code of goetta's origins.

But as I continued my journey, I realized that it would be next to impossible. The history was so far away, and recipes had been so muddled and adapted over the past 150 years. Few people would have clues. Did I expect to find that 175-year-old recipe carried over on the boat, written in Plattdeutsch and in Sutterlein (German cursive) script? Did that even exist? Most greater Cincinnatians can't speak High German, other than a few words, like *danke* and *prost*, let alone Plattedeutsch. Even fewer can read the old script. But I soldiered on, trying to collect what history I could.

Goetta has many ancestors from several different small regions in today's northwestern German states of Westphalia, Lower Saxony and Schleswig-Holstein. While I didn't find the exact village where goetta originated, I did discover a way to find out where a recipe may have originated based on some ingredients.

Today, you can determine how long goetta has been in a family by the way they pronounce it. My maternal grandmother pronounced it "gudda" and even spelled it "Guetta" on her recipe. She grew up in a small, one-and-a-half story shotgun Victorian with four siblings on Thornton Street, in the shadow of the Dorsel milling factory two blocks away, where the pinhead oats for goetta were processed and packed for retail sale to homemakers. Her aunt and godmother, Loretta Brosey Dorsel, was married to Jack Dorsel, the grandson of the founder of the Dorsel Pinhead Oatmeal Company, who had a love for old German sausage and, of course, goetta. I inherited furniture that Jack Dorsel made my grandmother, which I call my "goetta furniture." My grandmother's family also lived blocks away from the Corpus Christi Catholic Church among whose Germanic-immigrant parishioners were surely numerous recipes for goetta.

Some recipes I encountered in my search were clearly old. My grandmother had made several notes on how other family members made their goetta. She noted that her mother, Katherine Brosey Muchorowski, used pork flank, a cheaper, fatty, boneless portion of the pork belly between the ribs and the legs, with the beef. A note on the back of the recipe says that her sister's mother-in-law, Mrs. Westerkamp, used pork necks, which was a very old version. No one today would spend the time

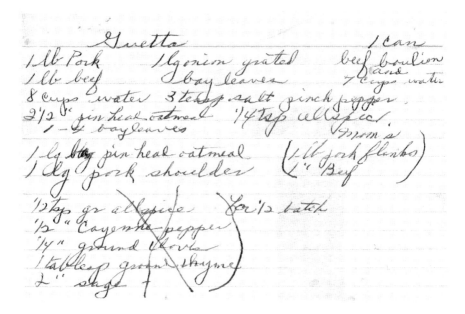

The "Guetta" recipe of Loretta Muchorowski Ling, spelled as many early Cincinnatians pronounced it. *Author's collection.*

to cook the pork necks and then pick the meat off the bone. But back in the day, that was a cheap cut, and it was worth the time for a German hausfrau. Grandma would not have had the time to cook and strip bones like that as she helped her husband run their bakery, but she made the note to document why Mrs. Westerkamp's goetta was so good. She did that on all of her recipes.

The Mrs. Westerkamp my grandmother referred to was her sister Mary Muchorowski Westerkamp's mother-in-law, Christina Westerkamp. Christina's parents were from Alsace-Lorraine, which is southwest of the Germanic goetta region, but the family of her husband, Oscar Sr., were butchers from Bavaria. Alex Westerkamp had immigrated just in time to fight in the Civil War and then operated a retail and wholesale butcher shop in the Pearl Street Market that his son Oscar Sr. and grandson Oscar Jr. "Bud" operated. So the recipe note using pork necks for goetta more likely came through Christina's line than her husband's Bavarian line, but she had access to whatever pork parts she desired from her husband's butchery. This genealogical work is what is necessary to trace the origin of an immigrant recipe, and it also can tell us how an original recipe evolved as it was passed down through the generations.

My paternal grandmother grew up in Covington, Kentucky. As the youngest of five girls, she learned how to cook later in life. Her goetta recipe was good enough for her father-in-law, whose wife's family had come from a farm in Oppenwehe, Westphalia, right in the center of the Goetta Cradle of Northern Germany, only ten miles to the west of Neunkirchen-Voerden, from where the Finke family, who claim to be the originators of goetta, hailed. When my grandparents moved into my great-grandfather's house after his wife's death to help out, he raved to the neighbors about his daughter-in-law's goetta and barley soup.

I created a Facebook group called "Cincinnati's Oldest Goetta Recipe." Within twenty-four hours, I had over two hundred members, and it now has over one thousand. Most members of this page are locals or expats who have moved out of greater Cincinnati and love and miss their goetta. The page has been a great way to crowdsource surveys on goetta. It became clear from those who submitted the legacy of their recipes that goetta probably originated with the immigrants of Covington from northwestern Germany and quickly made its way across the river before 1900, when it had made it to some of the meat markets at Findlay Market, like Wasslers and Eckerlein. The three oldest recipes submitted by people on the Facebook site had one thing in common: ancestors who came from Westphalia, Germany, and settled in Covington, Kentucky. Although the specific village of origin in Germany remains a mystery, I have narrowed the region of origin down to a parallelogram in northwestern Germany bounded by four cities: Munster, Oldenburg, Hamburg and Hanover. And, I learned a lot along the way of discovery about goetta.

I would like to thank the many people who contributed to the Big Goetta Project. Mark Balasa and Elmer Hensler of Queen City Sausage; Greg Langen of Langen Meats; Billy Finke; Jeffery Finke; Tom Dorsel; Gary Swaim, sales manager of Praire Mills; my high school friend Kyle Drahman, who bought Ammerland and Oldenburg pinkel and arranged a pinkel photo shoot with photographer Anatoli Weingart in Swabia, Germany; Doug and Melanie Nevluk of Maeker's Meats in Shiner, Texas; Dan Glier; my parents, Roger and Flora Woellert; Ted Swormstedt of the American Sign Museum; Kate Zaidan of Dean's Mediterranean, for inviting me to teach about the history and making of goetta at the inaugural STIR Immigrant Food at Findlay Kitchen and learning of goetta's similarity to Lebanese kibbeh; Polly Campbell, for finally getting me to taste Johnny-in-the-Bag sausage; Dick Stehlin; Jim Kluener of the Kluener Meats family; Sandy Hamilton, who carted livermush back from the Carolinas; Debby Van Dyke-Neubauer and her help with understanding the evolution of Dutch *balkenbrij*; the expert librarians at the Local History Department of the Downtown Public Library of Cincinnati and Hamilton County; the local history librarians at the Kenton County Public Library in Covington, Kentucky; my mother, for teaching me how to cook Crock-Pot goetta; and my maternal grandmother, Loretta Ling, for helping me understand how to distinguish "good gudda."

Chapter 1

PORKOPOLIS AND GOETTA

According to the Main Public Library of Cincinnati and Hamilton County on Vine Street, a large section of the Germanic-immigrant Over-the-Rhine neighborhood was known by the nickname "Goetta Alley," and Sander Packing was the first known commercial producer of goetta.

Goetta has evolved as cooking methods and appliances have. It originated as a by-product of slaughter, made over open fires in large pots, ground by hand. Before refrigeration, it was made only in the winter months and stored in crocks in pantries with a protective layer of congealed fat. Then came the pressure cooker, the electric meat grinder, the Crock-Pot, the gas grill, the microwave and, now, the air fryer. Along the way, goetta evolved with the use of better cuts of meat that were now more readily available. Instead of the pig head and organs, we started using pork shoulder and Boston butt and left out the organs. That's the product of it being a city grain sausage, rather than a country grain sausage. Cincinnati as a major metropolitan area had better access to better cuts of meat, more spices and more produce.

Goetta also has a pretty cool superpower that grain sausage cousins in Germany and the United States do not. It has its own built-in thermometer. When pinhead oats are heated, they pop, somewhat like popcorn. So if you're cooking goetta in a pan and the oats start to pop out of the patty, turn down the heat and cook slower. Take that, scrapple!

The pig is Cincinnati's spirit animal. And, as in Mexican folklore, the winged type is our *alebrijes*. ArtWorks Cincinnati, a nonprofit that uses the

An advertisement for Sander Packing, the first commercial producer of goetta in Cincinnati. *Courtesy of the Public Library of Cincinnati and Hamilton County.*

creation of public art as a vehicle to employ and train local artists and students, sponsored not one, but two Big Pig Gigs, in 2000 and 2012. These Big Pig Gigs placed nearly five hundred unique pig sculptures around town. After the gig, some of those pigs were auctioned and found permanent homes throughout the city: at the Shakespeare Theater; atop Queen City Sausage; the Superman Pig atop the SpringDot building off of I-75; inside Music Hall; Great American Ballpark, the Reds stadium; the Westin Hotel; the Moerlein Tap Room; Cincinnatus Pig at Sawyer Point; the Fortune Cookie Pig at Oriental Wok in Fort Mitchell; and PuckChop, the Hockey Pig at the U.S. Bank Arena. And the list goes on. Our city is even in its twentieth year of hosting the Flying Pig Marathon.

Even though goetta is a pork and beef grain sausage, the cow is not as much of an icon in Cincinnati as the pig. There is no flying cow equivalent to our flying pig city mascot. But there were nearly as many cows processed through our meatpacking houses as pigs. And Germanic immigrants found meat parts to make their goetta and take advantage of using everything but the oink or moo.

The place to start when looking for goetta in greater Cincinnati is Findlay Market. Located in the Germanic settled Over-the-Rhine neighborhood, it is our city's oldest continually operating market, opened in 1855. It is the last of nine public markets operating in Cincinnati in the nineteenth and early twentieth centuries. While originally almost every meat stall in the market had its own goetta, today, there are only three meat stalls that sell their own goetta: Eckerlin's, Grandma Debby's and Grayson's/Mike's Meats. And each uses very old recipies. It's still the highest concentration of suppliers you'll find in the area. Imagine nine city markets at the turn of the nineteenth century, each with their collection of Germanic butchers who each had a version of goetta or oatmeal sausage at their stall.

When our meatpacking history is considered, many look to Kahn's, which was most recently Cincinnati's largest pork producer. Many remember the "weiner the world awaited." Oddly enough, for as much

A scene of hog butchering from the 1920s in Green Township, Cincinnati. *Courtesy of the Public Library of Cincinnati and Hamilton County.*

meat as Kahn's processed, it never made a goetta product. But its 1932 cookbook, *American Beauty Meat Recipes*, had an interesting recipe for "American Beauty Pure Pork and Rolled Oats." It had no onions and was spiced with only salt and pepper, but it was cooled in pans, sliced, breaded and panfried, similar to goetta.

Kahn's Meats was founded by Elias Kahn, an immigrant from Albersweiler in the Rheinish Palatinate region of Germany. Immigrating to Cincinnati in 1882 with his wife and nine children, he started his meatpacking business in 1883 on Central Avenue. After his death in 1899, his four sons—Albert, Eugene, Louis and Nathan—took over the business. The company thrived for over eighty years. But in 1966, it was sold to Consolidated Foods Corporation, run by its Sara Lee Division. While Sara Lee kept the Kahn's brand, it stopped producing the local Kahn's favorite Germanic products, like Dutch loaf, Olive loaf deli meats and the local sausages, streamlining its product into more of a national, Americanized taste, rather than our local, heavily Germanic tastes. The large Kahn's plant in Cincinnati, which had employed so many, finally closed in 2006 and was demolished.

In 1833, more than eighty-five thousand pigs were processed in Cincinnati, and by 1844, twenty-six different meat-processing plants were located here. Cincinnati was the biggest city in the West by 1850 and quickly earned the nickname "Porkopolis." Cincinnati pork packers in the 1860s even pioneered the disassembly lines that represent the first modern production lines. The innovations of the disassembly line were keeping the carcass moving, eliminating downtime and synchronizing workers' movements. It was slaughterhouse production lines like these in Cincinnati that were copied by Chicago meatpackers and inspired Henry Ford to create his automotive assembly lines.

The availability of pork by-products brought other industries to the booming city. Small companies sprang up to process the by-products into soap and candles, including a little company called Procter & Gamble, which has branched out quite a bit since its founding in 1837.

But the pork industry, while profitable, wasn't always pretty. The Miami and Eire Canal ran red with blood from the nearby slaughterhouses, and German immigrants came home from the packinghouses covered in blood. There was no need for trash collection; swine roamed the sidewalks in the Packing House District, eating all the debris. Many visitors to antebellum Cincinnnati complained about the plethora of pigs and their accompanying filth.

Cincinnati remained high on the hog until 1862, until the Chicago Big Four meatpackers—Armour, Swift, Cudahy and Wilson—took the lead in pork production. With the Civil War underway, Cincinnati could no longer use the Mississippi River and its canals as a delivery route. Chicago, with its superior rail system, could deliver huge quantities of "the other white meat" to Union troops more quickly. To remain competitive, some of Cincinnati's pork investors organized the Cincinnati Union Stock Yards Company in 1871, a fifty-acre facility that could hold seventy-five thousand animals, including hogs, cattle, sheep and goats. Four other leading companies followed suit in the next two years, building adjoining stockyards. Despite the city's efforts, Chicago retained the edge. After 1920, pig packing numbers started to drop off, and the Cincinnati Stockyards finally closed on December 5, 1980.

There was even a local breed of hog, the Poland China Hog, which was bred in rural southwestern Ohio's Butler County, with sturdy bones and excess fat to handle the stroll to Cincinnati slaughterhouses. The original mother of the breed, Lady Pugh, was the first pedigreed Poland China Hog. She was born in 1865, bred by J.B. Pugh of Franklin, Ohio, her mother being the Old Harkrader Sow, owned by John Harkrader. Her sire was Bob. She was sold in 1868 to William Cheeseman Hankinson, who is given credit for starting the breed on his Pleasant Hill Farm in the now-

An 1888 stock certificate for the Union Stockyards of Cincinnati. *Courtesy of Jim Kluener.*

forgotten hamlet of Blue Ball, Ohio. He bred Lady Pugh for eleven years until her death, creating what is known as the Pleasant Hill Herd. The pedigreed pigs had great names, being named after famous writers, English nobility, American politicians, Native American chiefs, abolitionists and family members. One of Lady Pugh's progeny was a sow named Lady Butler, after Butler County, Ohio.

A discreet and nearly hidden site near the location of the original Pleasant Hill Farm has America's only monument to a pig. It's definitely worth a visit to the monument for those insatiable pork historians. The inscription on the monument reads:

> *The first pedigree of a Poland China Hog was written on this farm in August 1876, by W.C. Hankinson, owner of farm and Carl Freigau, compiler of the original record. This strictly American breed of swine originated within a radius of a few miles of this place, and in the making occupied the period from 1816 to 1850. The first volume of pedigrees was printed in 1878. This monument was erected by the Ohio Poland China Breeders Associations. Unveiled, June 15, 1922.*

LADY PUGH At 11 Years.

Bred by Brook Pugh, Property of W.C.Hankinson

Blue Ball O.

A sketch of Lady Pugh, the mother of the Poland China Hog breed. *Courtesy of the Warren County Historical Society Museum.*

The monument was originally located on the border of the Pleasant Hill Farm, one mile north of the village of Blue Ball, but it was moved in 1976 to its current location, across from Towne Mall. An opening was left in the foundation for a copper box containing a duplicate of the first pedigrees printed and other valuable articles sealed inside. Poland China Hogs are derived from many breeds, including the Berkshire and Hampshire. It is the oldest American breed of swine. The hogs are typically black, sometimes with white patches, and are known for their large size. Big Bill, the largest hog ever recorded, was a Poland China. It makes one wonder what Poland China Hog goetta tasted like.

By 1895, Cincinnati could brag of approximately forty-eight pork and beef packers and sixty slaughterhouses. Imagine all the cattle and swine needed to supply that amount of industry! Companies like H.H Meyer, the Cincinnati Abattoir Company and the Jacob Packing Company dotted the industrial landscape and made Cincinnati a major pork and beef slaughtering center. Camp Washington, with its central location and easy access to stockyards, railroad and the canal was where Cincinnati meat men congregated their businesses and made their fortunes.

The Camp Washington meat packers were Kluener Meats, Kahn's (517–523 Livingtston Street), William G. Rehn's Sons (452–454 Bank Street), Schlachter (2831–2841 Colerain Avenue), J.&F. Schroth (Massachusetts Avenue and Township Street), Jacob Bauer (2870 Massacheusetts), Ehrhardt (545 Poplar Street), Herman Kemper & Sons (2900 Sidney), Sam Gall, (2121 Freeman Avenue), Lohrey (2827 Massacheusetts), Gus Juengling & Son (2869 Massacheusetts) and Runtz.

Each meatpacking company had its own brand. Liberty Brand meats was a trademark of the Ideal Packaging Company; J. & F. Schroth had the Fountain Brand; Sander Packing—both pork and beef packers—had Morning Glory Brand and was credited with being the first commercial producer of goetta in Cincinnati; and Jacob Vogel & Sons had Star and Maple Leaf Brand meats. H.H. Meyer had Partridge, Golden Corn and Economy Brands. Kahn's meat brand was American Beauty.

After World War II, fifty meat plants closed in the Cincinnati area, twelve of those in Camp Washington. Kluener Meats, one of the last surviving, is a good example of how the meat companies were bought, closed and integrated into one another. Founded in 1895 by Joseph Kleuner Sr., the company passed through three generations of ownership. Kluener bought John Hilberg and Sons in 1969 and E.A. Kohl in 1988, which produced the Old World Brand of goetta. J. & F. Schroth packing closed in 1947. Kluener had been its distributor, so it took over beef slaughtering. Kluener hung on until closing in 1997.

Kluener was responsible for a local landmark familiar to many, visible from I-75 just south of Hopple Street, during its years of operation. Bossy, the Winking Cow sign, could be seen on the southbound side of the interstate at Camp Washington. It was such a local icon that, when mechanical problems shut down the wink, Kluener got calls from passersby that Bossy had stopped winking. The sign even got its own poem: "I'd never seen a winking cow, 'til Kluener's meats corralled one. But I can tell you anyhow, I'd rather see than be one."

Lohrey Packing closed in 1972 due to new USDA inspection regulations regarding pork processing. It was the last hog slaughterer and pork product supplier in Camp Washington. Founder Jacob Lohrey immigrated from Helsendorf, Hesse, to Cincinnati in 1852 as a child. He started the business in 1880 as a hog-slaughtering and smoked meats operation at 2827 Massachusetts Avenue. Lohrey had a great brand name for its meats, Brighton Belle, named for the old stockyards in Brighton, just north of Camp Washington. It consisted of bacon, skinless wieners,

A 1920s photo of Edward J. Kluener Sr. in front of his meat delivery truck. *Courtesy of Jim Kluener.*

smoked hams, boiled hams, luncheon meats, whole hog sausage and, of course, goetta.

By 1965, there were forty-one commercial meat businesses left in Cincinnati, including packers, sausage makers and slaughterhouses—less than half the number just sixty years prior. Today, only one of them is still standing, Queen City Sausage, which makes a line of great goetta products and carries the legacy of Cincinnati's Porkopolis days.

The burgeoning local restaurant scene and the demands of local chefs for heritage breeds of hogs have led to new livestock businesses like Queen City Livestock, a partnership between Chef Mike Florea and Jason Jones. These heritage breed hogs are being used for housemade goettas in local restaurants. Other farms like Finn Meadow Farms in Montgomery, Two Forks Farm in Mount Olivet, Kentucky, and Greenacres Farm in Cincinnati, are some of the local livestock companies providing heritage breed hogs to the area.

Chapter 2
GOETTA'S GERMAN ORIGINS

Goetta has come a long way since it traveled in steerage across the Atlantic with humble working-class German immigrants. Imagine you were leaving everything behind—your parents, siblings, maybe even your entire family—to come to America for better opportunity. You may have had nothing but the clothes on your back and a few *pfennig* in your hip pocket. But having the recipe for goetta, which you could make in America, with what ingredients were available, would remind you of your family, the parents you would never see again or the farm where you were raised. A simple food like goetta could remind you of home.

Many people who've traveled to Germany have said there is nothing like goetta that exists there—that goetta is a German-Cincinnatian concoction. That's simply not true. People have asked modern Germans if they've heard the word *goetta*, and a typical answer is no. That's because *goetta* is based on a hyperspecific regional Plattdeutsch dialect from a very specific region of northern Germany that is no longer spoken, or at least well known. It may have even been a nickname for a grain sausage from one small village. But if you ask a German if they have heard of different types of *gruetzwurst*, or grain sausages, like *knipp*, *pinkel* or *stippgruetze*, they will tell you yes—that's *Arme Leute Essen*, hillbilly food.

Saying "Well, I went to Germany, and they've never heard of goetta," is like living in Ohio your entire life and saying, "I've lived in the United States my entire life and never heard of a kolachi!" That's because you never traveled to central Texas, where the Czech Bohemians settled and where nearly every bakery makes kolaches. Similarly, unless you traveled to the farming region of northwestern Germany in Westphalia, Lower Saxony and the former Kingdom of Hanover, you wouldn't have run into a grain sausage similar to goetta, nor would another German know of it unless they lived or traveled there too. You will not find any forms of gruetzwurst in Germany at a soccer stadium, because they're just not popular enough. I went to a soccer game at Wolfsburg Stadium in Lower Saxony a few years ago. Wolfsburg is about an hour away from the current city of Hanover and right in the middle of the German "Cradle of Goetta," known for its variety of grain sausages. Even they had currywurst sausage for sale at the stadium, which was invented during the reconstruction after World War II in Berlin, which is about two and half hours to the east of goetta country. On the other hand, you will find goetta at the Reds' and Bengals' stadiums, because we have elevated this peasant food to a regional icon. If other grain sausages, like scrapple, are considered country sausages, then goetta is certainly a city grain sausage that was brought from the country.

It is more correct to say that goetta is a food form that existed for centuries in the farming regions of the northern Germanic kindgoms among the poorer classes. It was adapted to local ingredients easily obtained in Cincinnati. In recent decades, it has turned into an upscale regional breakfast treat. Indeed, in Cincinnati, there are three breakfast meats: sausage, bacon and goetta. But it was eaten at all meals in Germany, typically the afternoon meal. Its fattiness and extension with whole grains was meant to fuel a grueling twelve-plus-hour day working in the fields. The high fat content meant that it would keep without spoiling for many weeks in the colder winter months.

In Cincinnati, we've elevated goetta from a peasant food to a pop icon. In Germany, you'll be challenged to find these gruetzwursts in restaurants or at summer festivals outside of cities like Bremen, Hanover, Hamburg and Oldenburg, where they originated. But you will find them in the homes of farming people and at butchers in some of the regions.

In the farming regions of northwestern Germany, there is a long legacy of gruetzwurst or grain sausages. These were made at the time of slaughter in the fall, usually starting around St. Martin's Day, when temperatures were cooler. Today, starting in October, in the windows of local butchers in German goetta country, you'll see signs that read "Grutzwurst wieder vorratig" ("grutzwurst now in stock").

Historically, at slaughter time, after the prime cuts were taken—usually for the owner of the manor or for sale, and then the meats used for sausage—what was left was traditionally made into a grain sausage. This could have included the offal meats, or organs (lung, kidney, liver and heart), as well as other parts (the neck, tongue and head) of the hog and beef.

Sometimes, the blood was collected and made into a blood grain sausage. There are two families of grain sausages: those with blood and those without. Goetta, of course, falls into the non-blood-containing grain sausage. Goetta's local stepbrother, Johnny-in-the-Bag sausage, is an example of a grain sausage made with blood.

The slaughter of the pig in northern Germany was known as *Schlachtfest*. It was accompanied by a feast, which included sausages, blood wursts and goetta and its grain sausage cousins. It was accompanied by potatoes and sauerkraut. This is still a common event in the goetta country of Lower Saxony in Germany. Inns and organizations will buy a whole pig, slaughter it and have feasts to celebrate. One of Cincinnati's oldest German societies, the Kolping Society, celebrates an annual Schlachtfest.

But what exactly is goetta? That's the tricky part. It's been compared—incorrectly—to a lot of things. My least favorite description is "Cincinnati caviar." Goetta has been the victim of helicopter journalism, in which out-of-town journalists come in to try to describe it but miss the history and its nuances. Even respected food journalists have incorrectly said that some forms of goetta came to Cincinnati from the lower Rhineland of southern Germany.

The simplest way to describe it is a German breakfast meat similar to scrapple. In Cincinnati, there are three types of breakfast meats: sausage, bacon and goetta. But why is it always compared to scrapple? I would like to make it so that goetta is more widely known and so that scrapple is compared to goetta. Scrapple, as its name suggests, has more bits and parts than goetta does. In addition, pinhead oats are much healthier than cornmeal—more fiber and fewer complex carbs, so a much better glycemic index than scrapple.

Some have compared goetta to meatloaf. But it's not a meatloaf, because it has no more than a 50 percent meat-to-oats ratio, per USDA standards. Meatloaf is mostly meat with some bread crumbs thrown in as binder.

As goetta is fully cooked and put into bread pans to cure and coagulate, it somewhat resembles a terrine or forcemeat, which is a mixture of ground lean meat emulsified with fat, similar to a pâté. But although goetta does have fat, it has the pinhead oats, and forcemeats do not use a grain extender. Some have even compared goetta to a hash, but it contains no potatoes. Home recipes for goetta use straight muscle rather than organ meat like lungs, heart, kidney or even head meat. It's not a sausage, because it doesn't have the dense meat consistency of that food. So if it's not a sausage, not a meatloaf, not a hash and not a forcemeat, then what is it? Goetta is a gruetzwurst, which translates as "grain sausage."

The northwestern region of Germany can be called the "Cradle of Goetta," or, as the northwest Germans call it, "Grutzgraben," the crade of grain sausages. The region forms a sort of parallelogram from Munster in the southwest corner to Oldenburg/Bremen in the northwest corner, and from Hamburg in the northeast corner to Hanover in the southeast corner. If you split the parallelogram of this geography from Bremen to Hanover, you have two triangles. Goetta is believed to have come from the western of these two triangles, right in the center in a town called Neunkirken-Voerden. It was then carried over by the Finke family, which settled in Covington, Kentucky. Many immigrants in this area—then known as the Kingdoms of Hanover and Westphalia, and after World War II as Lower Saxony and Westphalia—came to Cincinnati and Covington and brought with them the tradition of these grain sausages.

These immgrants spoke slightly different regional dialects of Plattdeutsch, even though this region covers only a twenty-five-mile radius, which would

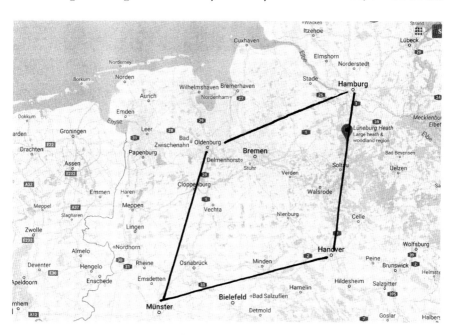

The map of the Cradle of Goetta in Germany. A parallelogram is formed by Munster, Oldenburg, Hamburg and Hanover. *Author's collection.*

fit into the Interstate 275 loop of greater Cincinnati. It would be like saying someone from Groesbeck has a different way of speaking English than someone from Hamilton. There are certainly neighborhood terms and words that might make the case for Cincinnati dialects. The terms *ponykeg* and *city chicken*, and the use of the word *please* as a question are hyperregional versions of what might be termed a Cincinnati dialect.

There are a few outlying regions from this cradle, like the state of Mecklenburg to the northeast of Hamburg, Ostfriesia to the north of Bremen and southern Netherlands provinces of Limburg, Brabant and Gelderland, which have their own grain sausages similar to goetta.

How these grain sausages were made depended on the landscape of the particular area or village. The meat could be pork, beef, mutton or a combination. For example, in the area of Lunenburg Heath, south of Hamburg, there is a grain sausage called *Heidjer Knipp*, made from the native sheep of that region. The grain could be oats, barley, rye or wheat. And whether or not onions were included depended on whether the region was boggy or marshy or had farmland capable of raising onions. Whatever meat was used, it was certainly a large slaughter animal whose leftover parts—like the head, neck and organs—were used to stretch out the whole animal. That's why you don't see other versions with nonslaughter animals like rabbit, raccoon or squirrel.

The spices were different across villages in this region. So, based on the known spice variations, we can make predictions on where your Germanic family came from based on your family's recipe. For example, if your family's goetta recipe contains garlic, cloves or marjoram, you are most likely descended from someone who came from Hesse and made *weckewerk*. If your goetta has only allspice, that ancestor most likely came from Hanover or Westphalia and made knipp or *stippgruetze*. If your goetta recipe doesn't have onions, you most likely came from the moors southeast of Hanover and made *hafer gritz*. If your goetta recipe has ginger, you most likely have an ancestor who came from southeast Holland and made *balkenbrij*. So take that, 23andMe—we don't need DNA testing to perform "recipe ancestry."

In the farm communities of northern Germany, most who worked them were known as heurling and were like peasants. They worked for the *Meier* or *Kolonus*, "master of the farm," who was the oldest male sibling born to the family. In Westphalia, for example, farmland was plotted out in the 1600s and was limited, so the farm would pass to the oldest son. All his siblings would basically be under his control and lived on the farm in small

A postcard showing the traditional costumes of some of the original goetta eaters from Westphalia. *Author's collection.*

cabins separate from the large house. They would have to ask permission to marry and were unlanded. Many of them took up other professions to supplement their sparse income after hours of working on the farm. Many learned to become weavers, potters or tailors. The lack of freedom is what motivated many of them to immigrate to America for better opportunities, especially after the rough conditions following the Napoleonic Wars. So they left the Cradle of Goetta and took with them their various recipes for their local grain sausage.

GOETTA'S GERMANIC ANCESTORS

The Practical Cookbook (*Praktisches Kuchbuch*), printed in 1874 in Leipzig, Germany, by Henriette Davidis, has a whole chapter of gruetzwurst recipes. It includes recipes for Mecklenburg-style gruetzwurst, *panhas* (made like Scrapple, but it uses buckwheat instead of cornmeal), *pinkelwurst* (just like goetta, only in sausage form), *sulze* (souse), *schwartenmagen/presskopf/presswurst* (head cheese) and *zungenwurst* (a cross between grain sausage and headcheese with blood, pickled tongue, oats and bread crumbs). The Mecklenburg

31

gruetzwurst is similar to goetta in that it's spiced with salt, pepper and allspice but also uses marjoram, which is not typically used in goetta. It also uses pearl barley instead of oats, uses blood and is pork only. Pinkelwurst, probably the closest recipe to goetta, calls for it to be served with stewed kale or with bean soup (more on that later). The book was reprinted in the 1890s as *The Practical Cookbook for Germans in America*. The popularity and wide use of this version is evidenced by the numerous secondhand copies still available.

The best explanation of goetta's ancestors is on the German website www. stippgruetze.de, which is dedicated to the preservation and education of the northwest German gruetzwursts. It is sponsored by a group founded in 2010 called IGITT (Interest Group of Traditional Teutonic Dishes), which travels the Cradle of Goetta—what they call "Grutzengraben," or "land of grain sausages"—and tastes various non-blood-containing gruetzwursts. Their goal is to introduce stippgruetze and other German regional grain sausages as worldwide staples and find the best through tasting all the regional varieties. That sounds a lot like the lofty goals of Glier's and Queen City Sausage. The group says Bavarians have their "Weisswurstequator," above which there is no weisswurst, and the northwest Germans have their Grutzengraben. Maybe Cincinnati's Glier's should team up with the IGITT for a joint Goetta-Gruetzwurst Fest.

Several museums in northwestern Germany are worth a visit to learn about the culinary history of the region's grain sausage ancestors of goetta. The Westfalische Freilichtmuseum in Detmold, Westphalia, is an outdoor village, sort of like our Sharon Woods Historic Village. It is made up of farmhouses and other historic buildings relocated to the site. The Landesmuseum in Oldenburg, set in an old palace, describes the cultural and culinary history of the Oldenburg area. Cloppenburg, just south of Oldenburg, has a historic village like Detmold that also presents the culinary history of the region.

Because of the high fat content, gruetzwursts are considered a good base for alcoholic drinking. The Westphalians recommend a Westfalische Klarer beer out of a tin mug to accompany the eating of any gruetzwurst. Those around Hannover recommend eating gruetzwurst with a drink combination called Luttje Lage, which will be discussed later.

Westphalians even have taken their love of the grain sausage to a pizza with their "Westphalian Pizza." It is a medium-thick crust topped with Polish onions, French yogurt, Swiss cheese, Brandenburg cucumbers and Westphalian gruetzwurst. And Cincinnatians think we were the first to invent goetta as a pizza topping!

There is a German word, *placken*, that describes the crisp outer crust that is required of panfried German grain sausages. Greater Cincinnatians know that crispy panfried is the required way to eat goetta. That being said, there are regions within the Cradle of Goetta where grain sausages are eated more loose, rather than pattied, and on toast, like an open-faced sandwich.

Bremen in the northwest corner of the Cradle of Goetta is the home of Germany's most widely known gruetzwurst, called knipp. It is made from pork head meat, pork belly, skin, pork or beef liver, broth, lard and onions and is seasoned with salt, allspice and pepper. Recipes vary, and it is sold either as *stange* (thick sausages) or *rolle* (wide) slices, like goetta. For breakfast in Bremen, knipp is served with a type of German biscotti called *zweiback*. This Bremen specialty is a zweibeck made out of twice-cooked brown bread and called *pferdefuss*, or horses' hoof. Knipp is also typically served with fried potatoes, scrambled or fried eggs, sour pickles, pickled beets, sweet and sour cucumber salad or sweet and sour bean salad.

In Westphalia, one form of knipp is known as Wesfalische Rindwurst and made from beef only, using pearl barley or oats. Stippgrutze is another version of knipp in the Minden-Lubbeke area of Westphalia that uses both pork and beef, with organ meats like heart, kidney or liver. It sometimes contains finely chopped onions, uses barley and is very high in fat. It is typically spiced with thyme and allspice. Most prefer it *placken*—panfried crispy.

Even where the sausage has been a staple for centuries, the same issues with appearance and mystery of ingredients plague newcomers from eating stippgrutze, as a translated article in the Minden, Westphalia daily newspaper from November 2017 explains:

> *The shorter the days, the larger the hunger for something hearty. In the area of Minden, that means it's time for stippgruetze! But such a dish is polarizing. Its biggest fans must admit that the East Westphalian specialty is not handsome. The approximately twelve centimeter long plastic intestine contains the gray solid mass, which originally consisted of leftover slaughter meats, barley groats and spices. When it's sizzling in the pan, some are wriggling their noses, while others mouths are watering.* (Mindener Tagenblatt, *November 11, 2017*)

However, those who love stippgruetze may take it to an even higher level than we do with goetta. In addition to the IGITT websiste, there is a stippgruetze fan page on Facebook, and last year, a German company offered a stippgruetz Advent calendar with small glass jars of regional gruetzwurst and sausages. This is applaudable, as neither Glier's nor Queen City Sausage has done a goetta Advent calendar.

In Oldenburg, knipp is known as *hackgrutt* or *hackgruetze* and served with blood sausage called *beutelwurst*. Buetelwurst—*buddelwurst* in Plattdeutsch—is a grain sausage containing blood that uses buckwheat or rye instead of oats, and usually has bacon.

In Osnabrück, knipp is known as *wurstebrei* or *wurstebrot*, which translates to "sausage bread." It's made with blood, bacon, pork and rye and uses wheat flour and spices. This sausage is a typical food from the Osnabrück region and is served with sliced bread and fried with lard or butter.

Also in Osnabrück is a loose form of gruetzwurst called *stopsel*. It is sautéed in the pan and served with bread or cooked and eaten with potatoes and beetroot. Ingredients of this dish are pork (including cooked pig's head and pork pork), broth and grits.

Near the current city of Hanover, knipp is known as *Calenburger pfannenschlag*, or *pannenslag* in the local Plattdeutsch. Calenburg is the rural region just to the southwest of the urban center of Hanover. It's a particularly fatty greutzwurst made from both beef and pork. It's flavored with clove, allspice, ginger, mace and cilantro and eaten with bread or potatoes and fried eggs or pickles.

In the region of Luneburger, *heide* (heath) knipp is made from the meat of a moorland sheep raised in that area. Pinkel, a sausage very similar to goetta, comes from Hanover, Oldenburg, Munster and Ammerland and is made of beechwood-smoked pork and beef, onions and oats. It is very popular in the fall and served as *Pinkel mit Kohl*, or "pinkel with the local kale."

In the fall, groups around Hanover have *Kohlfahrts*, or kale outings, where groups start at a meetup spot and parade to the local tavern, stopping along the way to play drinking games, and ending for a meal of local pinkel and kale at the inn or tavern. The tradition was started by the Oldenburg Turnerbund, a sport and social group founded in 1859 that also came to Cincinnati with Germanic immigrants in 1848. Some Kohlfahrt celebrations award a medal consisting of a cooked pork jaw on a chain, called the *Fressorden*, to the one who eats the most, crowning him "kohlkonig." The meal is accompanied by a local drink called *Luttje Lage*, which is a double shot—in two separate shotglasses simultaneously—of corn schnapps and local sour, top-fermented wheat beer like Herrenhauser. It takes quite a learned skill to successfully take this shot. Otherwise, the drinker is doused in alcohol.

An image of canned knipp, a goetta ancestor made by Bley in Ammerland, Germany. *Author's collection.*

The only city in the United States that stages yearly Kohlfahrts is Rochester, New York. The historic Genesee County Village and Museum hosts an annual Kohlfahrt. A two-hour guided nature walk of the museum grounds, complete with booze wagon and games, like a brussel sprout–shooting contest, is topped off with a hearty *Grunkohlessen* meal. Genesse County, New York, was home to a great deal of Germanic immigrants around the time of the Civil War. Maybe our city's German American Citizens League would consider hosting a Kohlfahrt in the future.

In Hamburg, in the German state of Schleswig-Holstein, knipp contains raisins and is called *rosinengruetzwurst*. It comes in a light goetta-like form without blood and one with blood. It is fried and served with the local sour Altenlander apples or stewed pear, and onions, with a side of freshly grated horseradish. This version of knipp can be found on the menu at several upscale eateries in Hamburg. The Restaurant Papillon at the Hotel Engel serves Holsteiner gruetzwurst with a dish called Heaven and Earth and *speckstippe*, a type of local bacon.

Germans understand digestion, and because of the high fat content of their gruetzwurst, they typically serve it with a side dish that is acidic to help break down the fat. Typical acidic accompaniments are sour pickle,

Pinkel sausage from Ammerland, packaged (*top*) and plated (*bottom*). *Courtesy of Kyle Drahman and photographer Anatoli Weingart.*

sweet and sour pumpkin, applesauce, stewed apples or pears, sauerkraut and beetroot. It is then served with a starch, like fried potatoes, or on brown bread or rye bread.

Throughout Westphalia and Lower Saxony, a popular gruetzwurst dish is called *Himmel und Erde* ("heaven and earth"). It consists of fried knipp, fried onions, potatoes and apple sauce. The *heaven* is for the apple, and *earth* is for the potato.

Another dish that consists of gruetzwurst with blood, in the sausage form, that is fried and split open is called *Tota Oma*, or "dead grandma," referring to its nonappetizing look. It is also called *Verkehrunsfall* ("traffic accident"), again, because of its slightly jarring appearance.

GRUETZWURST OF HESSE

Weckewerk is a gruetzwurst from the North Hesse region of Germany, near Hanover, just outside of the Cradle of Goetta. It is made from cooked skin and minced meat and pork meat or sausage broth, sometimes with boiled cuts of meat, blood and offal. The sausage is stretched with stale bread rolls, from which it gets its name. *Wecke* or *wegge* is the traditional name for the local *brotchen* or bread rolls in northern Hesse. This is the same roll that was imported to Buffalo, New York, and is used in the regional specialty sandwich Beef and Weck. The Amerian Buffalo wings chain BW3 is actually an abbreviation of Buffalo Wild Wings and Weck. The weck is also where the caraway comes from in the spice blend used for making weckewerk. It is also seasoned with onions, salt, pepper, marjoram, clove, pepper and garlic. The ingredients are mixed together and then run through a meat grinder. If it is to be eaten within a week or so, weckewerk comes stuffed in pig's stomach. For longer storage, it is preserved in jars or boiled in larger synthetic casings.

Just like other grain sausages, weckewerk or *weckwurst* is fried in the pan. The former mayor of Kassel, Germany, Philipp Scheidemann, likes his weckewerk almost burned, and this form of preparation is called "*Mayor Art.*" Common side dishes are boiled potatoes, pickled cucumbers and beetroot or a green salad with smoked sauce.

In addition to *ahlen wurscht*, liver sausage and blood pudding, the weckewerk is one of the standard products of traditional home slaughtering in northern Hesse. It was originally a way to use up the leftovers from the slaughter, like goetta.

THE GRAIN SAUSAGES WITH BLOOD

The grain sausage containing blood is not as popular now as it once was in greater Cincinnati. This is a family of grain sausages similar to our Johnny-in-the-Bag, which is now only produced seasonally by Stehlin's Meats.

In northwest Germany, these blood grain sausages are called *wurstebrot* and are from the area of Osnabrück and Münster. They are made from blood, rye meal, fatty bacon, pork, flour and spices. To make fresh, still warm blood from the slaughtered animal is mixed with the meat broth, grains and minced pork and seasoned spicy. It's poured into loafs and then panfried.

When slaughtering on a farm, a number of these blood grain sausage loaves used to be produced and stored. To prepare the actual sausage bread, or a *wourstbrotssoppen*, the chopped loaves with boiled bacon were cooked to a porridge and eaten especially, for breakfast. Often, sausage bread is sliced together with *leberbrot* ("liver bread") in thick slices and eaten fried in the pan. Some regions replace liver bread with apple slices as an accompaniment. Slices of sweet apple varieties like "Dülmener Rose" are fried in the pan with the blood sausage.

In the different regions of northwestern Germany, very different names have developed for these blood grain sausages. The recipes also vary slightly from village to village in the amount of blood included, the type of grain and flour content and the spices used. The name in South Westphalia is *mopkenbrot*; in Westphalia, it is *wobkenbrot*; in Artland, it is *wobkebraut*; in the Rhineland, it's *panhas*; and in the three provinces of southeast Holland, it's known as *balkenbrij*.

THE GOETTA OF VAN GOGH

Balkenbrij is one of the goetta ancestors that is native to the southeastern provinces of the Netherlands, Limburg, Brabant and just to the west of the far corner of the Cradle of Goetta. It translates from the Dutch to "belly porridge." It's prepared with the pluck—heart, liver, lungs and kidneys—along with other leftover meat from the pig, and sometimes blood. It is then cooked, ground and cooked again, with bacon and some sort of grain, which varies from buckwheat to rye.

Because of the high content of organ meat, a special local spice blend is used, called *rommelkruid*, which consists of ground licorice, sugar, anise, clove, cinnamon, white pepper, ginger and sandalwood—think of German gingerbread spices. Goetta typically only used allspice to counter the minerally organ flavor when it used those cuts in its early days.

The Limburg.ne website says balkenbrij in Limburg "is a delicacy that should not be absent from any Christmas breakfast, and to make it without blood is unthinkable." Ok, so that made it into our family—no Christmas breakfast at home is without goetta. Balkenbrij was so popular in the old days that, during Lenten fasting, a meatless variety was made with pork stock. After being poured in loaf pans and gelled, the delicacy is cut in slices one centimeter thick and panfried, usually in ox fat, the staple fat of the region, until "brown and crispy."

Balkenbrij is also eaten in variation in the two provinces that border Limburg. Gelderland, to the east, doesn't use blood. But they do sweeten it up with the use of raisins, currants or other local sweet berries. Their sweeter variety is served with sugar, or a sweet syrup called treacle, over pancakes. The more savory Limburg version is served, like goetta, as a meat substitute and with a good rye bread.

The rural farm province of Brabant to the east makes a much simpler version, probably because of the expense of the spices. In Germany, across the border from Limburg, pearl barley is used instead of buckwheat or rye in their variant of balkenbrij, which is called *moppkenbrot*.

Brabant is where the famous Dutch impressionist Vincent van Gogh was raised and started his career. Although the majority of his famous paintings are in the Van Gogh Museum in Amsterdam, he spent the 1880s sketching the rural farmers—the balkenbrij eaters—of Brabant. His first masterpiece, *The Potato Eaters*, shows a family of Brabant farmers sitting to a modest dinner. That painting should really be named *The Balkenbrij Eaters*! A local van Gogh tour in Brabant has a day of regional cooking of foods from the days of Van Gogh, with regional chefs, and it features a balkenbrij tasting. So van Gogh subsisted on this wonderful grain sausage as he painted what would become million-dollar artworks. That's pretty good for a peasant.

Today, according to the website, there are only fifty butchers in Gelderland that make balkenbrij, and twenty or so in Limburg and Brabant combined. A 1995 campaign in the Netherlands called "Tafelen in Nederland" ("Dining in the Netherlands") tried to revive regional home cuisine, like balkenbrij, with the younger generations, serving elevated dishes like "wild boar and balkenbrij in puff pastry." But sadly, interest in balkenbrij in the Netherlands is decreasing, because, like goetta, it is a long, laborious, many-hours process to make.

Balkenbrij made it to America in the large areas of Dutch immigration in and around Holland, Michigan, and Zeeland, Michigan, where it's eaten in an Americanized form on a small scale.

A good friend of mine, Debby, grew up on balkenbrij in her native Amsterdam and shared with me her mother's balkenbrij recipe, for comparison to goetta. She said that, growing up, balkenbrij was a "Friday night comfort food."

The recipe is a mix of Brabant and Gelderland styles.

Mevrouw van Dijk's Balkenbrij

500 grams pork (in general, all types of scrap meat is fine for this, organ parts as well)
100 grams fatty bacon
15 grams mixed spices (thyme, bay leaves)
2 cubes beef boullion
1 liter water
Pepper
250 grams buckwheat flour
75 grams raisins (let them sit in water overnight)
¼ liter pig's blood
Butter for baking

Put all the meat in one pot and boil. Add spices, pepper and boullion cubes and water, place on low heat for 40 minutes. Take the meat out and cool down broth. Sift the broth. Cut the meat in small pieces or put through the meat grinder. Take 1/3 of the broth and mix it with the flour. Boil the meat with the remainder of the broth and add the raisins and blood. Keep stirring, and add the flour mixture slowly. Boil for another 15 minutes and keep stirring. You will get a stiff mixture. Dump the mixture in a bowl that has been cooled down by mixing it with cold water. Leave it in the fridge overnight. Then cut into thick slices and fry in the pan with butter.

SCOTTISH HAGGIS

Haggis is certainly not a German grain sausage. But it's one of the few grain sausages that utilizes oatmeal and is similar to goetta. The Scottish have long eaten cooked oatmal—and were ridiculed for it by the English, who said oats were suitable only for horses. Food historians in Scotland think that its origin came from the continent, perhaps in northwestern Germany or farther south. Haggis is made of a sheep's heart, lungs and liver, as well as onions, oatmeal and spices. It is stuffed into the sheep stomach, boiled, sliced and fried crispy like goetta. I ate haggis on a business trip to Scotland several years ago, and I can attest to it tasting and looking very similar to goetta.

SWEDISH PÖLSA

Although also not German, it is important to mention *pölsa*, northern Sweden's traditional grain sausage. The dish's name derives from the Norwegian and Danish word for sausage, *polse*. Its main ingredients are liver, heart, onion, pearl barley and also ground beef or minced pork, mixed with stock, black pepper and marjoram. It is usually served with boiled or fried potatoes, pickled beetroot and sometimes a fried egg.

The dish makes it into Swedish pop culture as a central role in Torgny Lindgren's allegorical novel *Hash* (*Pölsan*), in which two men go on a personal quest across postwar Sweden in search of the genuine Swedish pölsa. Denmark has popularized this grain sausage via food trucks that offer it as the "Copenbagen Street Dog."

All of these European grain sausages bring us to what I call the Goetta Family Tree. Like a human family tree, the Goetta Family Tree shows us the grain sausages from which our goetta descends and its closely related food cousins. The ingredients, spices and cuts of meat are like DNA that connect each grain sausage to their individual region of origin. It helps us to understand that goetta it not just a Cincinnati thing but a descendant of a long heritage of grain sausages in northern Europe.

GOETTA ETYMOLOGY

There have been many explanations of where the name *goetta* came from. It is certainly a Plattdeutsch word, and a regional dialectual Plattdeutsch word at that. It does not come from the High German (*Hochdeutsch*) of

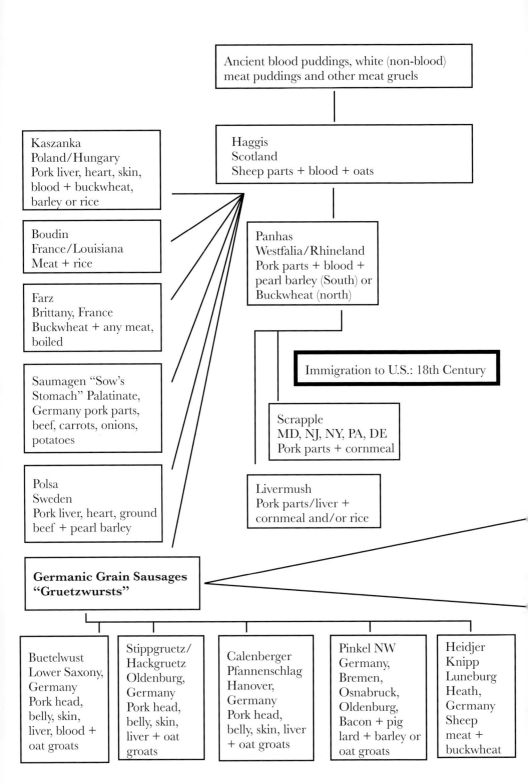

Ancient blood puddings, white (non-blood) meat puddings and other meat gruels

Kaszanka
Poland/Hungary
Pork liver, heart, skin, blood + buckwheat, barley or rice

Haggis
Scotland
Sheep parts + blood + oats

Boudin
France/Louisiana
Meat + rice

Panhas
Westfalia/Rhineland
Pork parts + blood + pearl barley (South) or Buckwheat (north)

Farz
Brittany, France
Buckwheat + any meat, boiled

Immigration to U.S.: 18th Century

Saumagen "Sow's Stomach" Palatinate, Germany pork parts, beef, carrots, onions, potatoes

Scrapple
MD, NJ, NY, PA, DE
Pork parts + cornmeal

Polsa
Sweden
Pork liver, heart, ground beef + pearl barley

Livermush
Pork parts/liver + cornmeal and/or rice

Germanic Grain Sausages "Gruetzwursts"

Buetelwust
Lower Saxony, Germany
Pork head, belly, skin, liver, blood + oat groats

Stippgruetz/ Hackgruetz
Oldenburg, Germany
Pork head, belly, skin, liver + oat groats

Calenberger Pfannenschlag
Hanover, Germany
Pork head, belly, skin, liver + oat groats

Pinkel NW Germany, Bremen, Osnabruck, Oldenburg, Bacon + pig lard + barley or oat groats

Heidjer Knipp
Luneburg Heath, Germany
Sheep meat + buckwheat

THE GOETTA FAMILY TREE

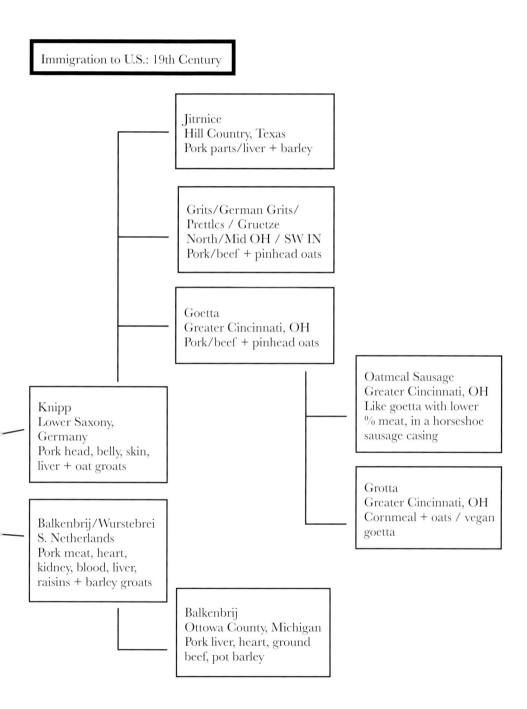

Immigration to U.S.: 19th Century

Jitrnice
Hill Country, Texas
Pork parts/liver + barley

Grits/German Grits/
Prettles / Gruetze
North/Mid OH / SW IN
Pork/beef + pinhead oats

Goetta
Greater Cincinnati, OH
Pork/beef + pinhead oats

Oatmeal Sausage
Greater Cincinnati, OH
Like goetta with lower
% meat, in a horseshoe
sausage casing

Grotta
Greater Cincinnati, OH
Cornmeal + oats / vegan
goetta

Knipp
Lower Saxony,
Germany
Pork head, belly, skin,
liver + oat groats

Balkenbrij/Wurstebrei
S. Netherlands
Pork meat, heart,
kidney, blood, liver,
raisins + barley groats

Balkenbrij
Ottowa County, Michigan
Pork liver, heart, ground
beef, pot barley

today's unified Germany. The original immigrants from northwestern Germany spoke Plattdeutsch and the dialect of their small regions or even smaller towns and villages. These hyperregional dialects still exist in Germany today. One can order a *halbe*, or half glass of beer, at a bar in Swabia in south Germany, and in less than a few miles cross the border into the state of Bavaria, where the same half glass is called a *helles*. The Bavarian bartender will know what a halbe is but will also know that you are definitely not a Bavarian.

The most common explanation in Cincinnati is that *goetta* comes from the West Munster dialectual Plattdeutsch word *grötte*, or *groetta*, for the High German word *gruetz*, which means "grain." That may be plausible, but why would the *r* be somehow dropped? And why would Germans just say "grains" for a specific grain sauage that contains oats? That would be like us saying we'd like to have a bowl of grains when referring to our morning bowl of hot oatmeal.

We know two things about Germans and their words. First, they like to be descriptive, especially about their food. This descriptiveness results in large words, called cognates, which are multisyllabic and combinations of several words. Second, we also know that Germans love to nickname their foods in funny or sometimes derogatory ways. Examples are *Tota Oma* ("dead grandma" in English) and *Verkehrunsfall* ("traffic accident"), both of which are nicknames for dishes with grain sausages.

In the Pinneberg area around the port city of Hamburg, the Plattdeutsch dialect for *gruetzwurst* is *gritwuss*. That might tell us where the term *grits* comes from. But we also know that when just *grits* is used to indicate a grain sausage, it is preceded by the word for the type of grain used. So, in this case, in U.S. Germanic immigrant communities like Minster, Ohio, and others, when *grits* was used to describe an oatmeal-based grain sausage, it was preceded by the word for oats, *hafer grits* (in High German), or *hobern grits/habern grits* (in the Plattdeutsch dialects of Kreis Verden and Lower Saxony, respectively, both of which are in the Goetta Parallelogram). A 1968 goetta recipe was described in the *Cincinnati Post Times Star* by Elizabeth Grote and purported to be her grandmother's that she brought to Cincinnati in 1868. She said their family called it "hafer grits." The recipe called for a decent amount of cooked bacon, along with the other pork and beef, which might indicate they came from the Osnabrück area of Germany.

Another word similar to *goetta* from the Ammerland Plattdeutsch dialect is *goert*, which means "gruetzwurst." Ammerland is the area in the Goetta

Parallelogram where another grain sausage, pinkel, is from. But then again we have the problem of why they would remove the *r*, and where is the "a" sound at the end of the word?

There is a Plattdeutsch word, *götte*, that comes from the north Elmsland dialect. North Elmsland borders Oldenburg on the western tip of the Goetta Parallelogram. That word means "pearl barley." That word would be pronounced as early Germanic Cincinnatians pronounced *goetta*, which is "gutta." And most of the grain sausages in the Goetta Parallelogram use barley as the grain and not pinhead oats. Perhaps originally goetta was *göttewuss* in northwestern Plattdeutsch country, a pork beef and barley grain sausage. When Cincinnati Germanic immigrants came to the area, unrolled pinhead oats were more readily available and cheaper than pearl barley, and thus the sausage was transformed. This is exactly what happened with the Pennsylvania Dutch's grain sausage scrapple. In Germany, called *panhascrapple* or *panhas*, it was made with buckwheat. When it came to America, milled cornmeal was more readily available and the grain change was made, but the name was not changed. This is certinaly my bet and the most logical explanation, given all the possibilities. But we may never know the answer. That smoking gun of a recipe, written in regional Plattdeutsch in old Germanic sutterlein script, noting the village from where the first goetta immigrant arrived, has yet to be found.

Whatever the specific origin, *goetta* became the word that Germanic immigrant greater Cincinnatians associated with the pork and beef pinhead oat grain sausage we now know and love. And that happened over decades in small Germanic neighborhood enclaves and butcher shops by word of mouth, not by over-the-top "Mad Men" guerilla marketing campaigns.

In urban Cincinnati or Covington, poor German immigrants who knew how to make gruetzwurst wouldn't have had whole pigs to slaughter, as they would have on the farm in Germany. But they would have access to the parts discarded by the local butchers and slaughterhouses on the cheap. Spareribs and pigs feet were common throwaway items that boardinghouses obtained in large quantities to cheaply feed their tenants. Immigrant housewives could get pig heads, feet, snouts and necks from these slaughterhouses or from hucksters who sold meat from their horse-drawn wagons door-to-door and near the many markets of Cincinnati: Court Street, Findlay and Fifth Street.

There are references that the Cincinnati German Ohio Ninth Regiment in the Civil War was known for its cooking prowess. When the non-German regiments cooked a pig, they roasted it whole on the spit, often not cooking it long enough to cook all the way through to the center. As a result, many of these regiments would suffer from food poisoning, and the entire regiment would be out of commission. The Cincinnati Germans were familiar with pig slaughter and broke down the whole pigs that they received for rations and cooked parts separately, ensuring they were cooked through. They never got sick and were consulted by the leaders of the Anglo regiments to understand how to more safely prepare their food. These are the Germans who knew how to use everything but the oink and who used the spare parts to make grain sausages like goetta.

If goetta landed first in Covington, how and when did it travel across the river to Cincinnati? Coppin's Hotel and Restaurant in Covington, Kentucky, has a great goetta dish they serve called Roebling Benedict. John Roebling was the German immigrant engineer who designed and oversaw the building of our John Roebling Suspension Bridge and later the Brooklyn Bridge. At the time, it was the only bridge that allowed free access from Cincinnati to northern Kentucky. I thought Roebling, at his office in Covington (which is now Roebling Points Bookstore), could definitely have fueled his long days overseeing the bridge construction with a breakfast of delicious goetta. And, was his ingenious suspension bridge responsible for the migration of goetta from its American birthplace in Covington to the large metropolis of Cincinnati?

While all Cincinnati Germanic immigrants didn't necessarily cluster in enclaves with others from their specific region in Germany, they did cluster by social organizations by region, particularly in their Beneficial Societies or *Unterstutzung-Vereine*—the early insurance companies. There were societies of Swiss, Baden, Bavarian and so forth. So a butcher would have to provide sausages that pleased the likes of the Bavarian, Baden, Hessian and Westphalian customers in his neighborhood all at once. So a sausage that was maybe a specialty in one region was enhanced to appeal to a broader palate. This is how the Bavarian Weisswurst morphed into the Cincinnati brat, and how the Nuremberger Mettwurst became our Cincinnati Smoked Mett. While this Germanic fusion made it easier for butchers across the city to sell to a larger customer base, it certainly makes it hard for us food historians to trace the exact path of goetta! So then *goetta* became the regional name for our local Germanic grain sausage. It gave one name that all Germanic immigrants could identify, even though it may have been slightly different, as it is today, across all the butchers and producers.

In the January 25, 1918 edition of the German newspaper the *Cincinnat Volksblatt*, Richard Gollmer wrote an article translated as "Facts about Sausage." The translation shows how many Germanic regional sausages were known to Cincinnati's Germanic immigrant community:

> *Who doesn't know the Wiener, Frankfurter, Regensburger, Halberstadter, Zauersche, Breslauer, Bock-, Rost-, Brat-, Gruetz-* [the category in which our goetta falls], *Pinkel-* [cousin of our goetta], *Blut-, Leber-, Cervelat, Schinken-, Schlack-, Mett-, Weiss-* [the ancestor of the Cincinnati brat], *Bier-, Bruh-, Knack-, Zungen-, Topf-, Sulzwurst, or for that matter, Schwartenmagen, Presskopf* [head cheeses], *Mortadella, or salami, and so forth?*

He goes on to say, "Sausage is not a new invention. The Romans had their sausage—Botellum, Tomaculum, Lucania (Bratwurst). The Galls had Hilla (Knockwurst). And the Anglo-Saxons had gruetzwurst (499 varieties)."

The last statement is very interesting. This German writer claims the ancient Anglo-Saxons, who resided in the northwestern coast of Germany near the Westphalian-Hanoverian-Saxony Cradle of Goetta, invented the gruetzwurst, or grain sausage. The Saxons would eventually invade what is now England and give it their ancient black and white puddings— grain sausages with and without blood, respectively. So perhaps *goetta* is even an ancient Anglo-Saxon term for a particular type of grain sausage. The "499 varieties" reference is interesting as well. As we see, there are many different types of gruetzwurst or goetta ancestors in the Cradle of Goetta, and each village probably has its specific variety of each. There are probably just as many variations on the goetta recipe.

Because of this variety, one can predict with a reasonable degree of certainty from an old goetta recipe which area of Germany that particular family came from, based on the ingredients of the hyperregional grain sausages. For example, if your family's goetta recipe came with garlic, cloves or marjoram, you are most likely descended from someone who came from Hesse (*weckebrot*). If your goetta has only allspice, that ancestor most likely came from Hanover or Westphalia (knipp/stippgrutze). Goetta recipes without onions most likely came from the cold, swamp region southeast of Hanover (hafer grits). If your goetta recipe has ginger or uses currants, you most likely have an ancestor who came from southeast Holland (balkenbrij). If your goetta recipe includes pig skins or cracklins, your family is probably of Ostfriesian origin. If your goetta calls for bacon along with other pork meat, your family likely came from the area around Osnabrük. And, if your goetta includes raisins, your family is definitely from Hamburg or the province of Schleswig-Holstein.

But now that we know goetta did originate in the Germanic Kingdoms of Hanover and Westphalia, and that it left behind a large family tree of gruetzwurst, we can begin its long journey to greater Cincinnati and its evolution in Porkopolis.

Chapter 3
THE ORIGINAL FINKE'S

I knew I had come to the right place when I arrived one Sunday afternoon at Finke & Sons in the hills of Lookout Heights, Kentucky, near Fort Wright. One of the butchers saw me with my green folder and said, "Oh, you're the goetta guy. Follow me." He led me behind the meat counter into the back room, where Billy Finke, the youngest of the sons of Finke & Sons, was making their prized goetta. The awesome smell of the room triggered memories of my mother and grandmother making "gudda" in their kitchens. The meat and the pinhead oats had been cooking separately already for many hours, and he was ready to grind the meat and mix it into the oats to show me the final steps in their process.

Billy had fried a slab of their goetta for me to taste and had a jar of maple syrup out for the dressing. I told him I came from a ketchup-dressed goetta family, but I wanted to taste it undressed to take in all the nuances of flavor. I took my first bite; it tasted just like my grandma's, except that she didn't grind the meat fine, and the bits of onions in hers were bigger. He also let me taste the goetta, when still warm, right after he mixed it, before pouring it into the pans, where it would "gel" into the slabs for frying.

He had brought his Uncle Jim, the oldest living of the original brothers, to answer my questions about the history of their family and its goetta production. When Uncle Jim said, "So, what do you want to know about our 'gudda'?," the ghosts of my ancestors sang a song of hallelujah in Plattdeutsch. He pronounced it just as both of my grandmothers, who were raised in Covington and Newport, Kentucky, had. This proved that he and

The sign for Finke's noting the Original Goetta. *Author's collection.*

his family were a true connection to the original recipe of goetta. It was like being admitted into a secret meeting of the Knights Templar. For the next hour and a half, Uncle Jim, a virtual oracle of goetta history, revealed secrets of early goetta production. With the large Catholic families of the Finkes, it takes a geneology chart and a guide like Uncle Jim to walk you through the history of the business as it progressed over the past 140 years.

Now, some of his older relatives who have gone to that Great Pinhead Oat Field in the Sky have claimed that the Finkes invented goetta. Uncle Jim said that the female relative who made the claim was a bit of a storyteller, and although not involved in the meat business, she always wanted to have her voice heard for posterity. And, as tall-tale-like as some of her oral history might be, it's appropriate that a woman's voice should tell the story of goetta. That's because the Finke goetta recipe is said to have started from Louise Reinersman Finke, the wife of Johann Gerhard, known in America as George Finke Sr. Together, the couple started a butcher shop in 1876 in Covington's heavily German neighborhood of Mainstrasse and Mutter Gottes. That is the oldest documentation of a business making goetta in greater Cincinnati.

So if the Finkes weren't the first to introduce the name and product of goetta in our area, they are the earliest producers that we know. And their story does follow the other oral histories we hear of German immigrant farm communities in America. The men butchered the hogs and cattle and made the sausage, while the women took the scraps and made their variety of grain sausages or gruetzwurst, of which goetta is a family member.

George and Louise had immigrated to Cincinnati from the Cradle of Goetta—a town then in the Germanic Kingdom of Hanover called Neunkirchen-Voerden. They arrived in Baltimore on the ship *Leocardia* from Bremen, Germany, on November 30, 1869, with others from the villages near it. Gerhard's occupation was listed as a butcher on the ship manifest. The only other head of a family listed as a butcher from the same village was Heinrich Roewer, who decided to stay in Baltimore instead of traveling to Cincinnati, as all the others planned. Baltimore had long been a haven for German Catholic immigrants, who were sort of the unicorns or rarity in the northern German Lutheran country of the Kindgom of Hanover. Most were Lutherans.

George and Louise stayed a few years in Cincinnati's densely populated West End after being married at St. Anthony's German Catholic Church on Budd Street. One of the early jobs George had was a furniture maker at the Mitchell and Rammelstein Furniture Company in Cincinnati. Their nine children would follow shortly, about one every other year, after they moved to Covington. And after settling and working odd jobs as a laborer and varnisher, George opened in 1876 a daily market at 634 Main Street and Sixth with his wife and his brother-in-law, Joseph Reinersman, who drove the truck for their meat delivery business. Joseph died in 1880, and in 1883, George erected a large three-story building at 824 Main Street, which became the shop and Finke family home for the next eighty years.

The Finkes were originally members of the German Catholic St. Aloysius Church, which used to stand on Seventh and Bakewell Streets. St. Aloysius Gonzaga is the patron saint of youth and those suffering from epidemics. St. Aloysius died while serving victims of an epidemic in Spain. Many local Germanic immigrants perished in the cholera epidemics in greater Cincinnati. So he is kind of an appropriate patron saint of goetta, as it was a dish that sustained the poor and destitute first-arriving Germanic immigrants to our area.

George Finke Sr. built an extensive brick summer kitchen that they called the Sausage Haus in the back of the Main Street store. The Sausage Haus served as storehouse, processing plant and smokehouse. Both buildings are still standing in the Mainstrasse neighborhood, where the original Goettafest started. George Finke Jr. carved his name in 1893 for posterity in the lintels of one of the windows of the smokehouse. Few of the revelers who eat or drink their way through the popular Mainstrasse entertainment district know that steps away is perhaps where goetta in greater Cincinnati was born. There should be an historical marker placed at this site so that goetta eaters can pay homage.

Louisa Finke's siblings had already come to Covington: her sisters Anna Maria and Theresia and brothers Bernhard and Joseph. Only Joseph was involved in the meat business. But there was certainly a growing chain-

The original smokehouse behind Finke's Meats on Main Street in Covington, where goetta was made. *Author's collection.*

immigrant community of Germanic goetta eaters forming in Covington. And the Irish working class was quick to catch on, too. There's a family story that George Finke Jr. tried to sell goetta from his meat-wagon route in the Irish immigrant neighborhood of Covington along Main Street near St.

Patrick's Catholic Church. When he told them it was called "goetta," they shied away from it, as they'd never heard of it. So he started calling it Irish Mush, and they bought in. The working-class Irish had a tradition of black and white puddings, similar to grain sausages like goetta. Black pudding was grain sausage with blood, white pudding without. These two Irish meat puddings are close cousins to the Scottish haggis, which uses sheep lungs, heart and liver, and onions and oatmeal, all stuffed into the stomach.

As with many goetta recipes, the Finkes' has been modified over the years. Uncle Jim says that, originally, they used all the scraps in the goetta. That meant that, in addition to the pork callie cut, or shoulder (also sometimes locally called the "picnic cut"), they used green (unsmoked) jowl bacon, pork snouts, hearts and beef tongue.

Today, their recipe calls for lean 90/10 meat/fat Boston butt pork; 80/20 beef. They use no allspice or garlic, and they grind the onions fine. Billy's cousin Jeffrey makes his own goetta, which he sells under the brand name Gourmet Goetta. Billy says his cousin doesn't grind his onions as fine, so the result is chunky bits of onion, which some people like. Billy also points out the fact that he cooks the meat and pinhead oats separately, all of which contribute to the flavor. They make regular, spicy and hot versions of their goetta, as well as a gluten-free version.

Billy made about twenty tons of goetta in 2017. He says he makes double the normal weekly amount during the holidays, especially Christmas, when families of German ancestry eat big holiday brunches together. Of course, it's nowhere as large as what Glier's in nearby Covington makes, but it's the greatest volume of any of the singular meat markets in greater Cincinnati.

Apparently, Louise Finke was a tough one. After her husband died early of blood poisoning in 1888, she took over the butcher shop and butchered the meats herself. She did, according to family lore, have help from the fireman across the street at Covington Company No. 4 when she bought beef directly from the droves being led down Main Street to the Lewisburg slaughterhouses.

In a tragic end to the Goetta Queen, Louise Reinersman Finke was killed by a motorist walking home one rainy Sunday afternoon in 1930 coming home from St. Aloysius. It was rumored that the motorist who hit her, Kueckle, had been drinking, but no charges were ever brought against him.

Although it was through George Jr.'s line that the business continued, one sister, Irene Finke, and her husband, Ray Klug, operated a meat market at Seventeenth and Garrard Streets in Covington, where her brother Pat Finke operated the meat counter.

Billy Finke making the weekly goetta at the Fort Wright meat market. *Author's collection.*

1876 Recipe Still Used

Mike Finke, grandfather of Billy Finke, stirring goetta. *Courtesy of Kenton County Kentucky Public Library.*

A FRESH BATCH — Mike Finke, Covington's leading goetta maker, emerges from his smokehouse, left, with a nicely-smoked stick of goetta sausages. At right, he's at the 60-gallon kettle he uses to mix and cook the ingredients.

Elmer "Mike" Finke, a grandson, took over the 824 Main Street Store in 1936. He continued making the old German products like schwartenmagen (head cheese), souse (spicy head cheese), a beutelwurst (a blood sausage made with buckwheat instead of pinhead oats) called Johnny-in-the-Bag and, of course, goetta. They even made a smoked link version of goetta, similar to pinkel in Germany.

Mike's brothers carried on the meat-route business, like their father, George Jr., had done, while their mother ran the butcher shop. Henry ran routes in Erlanger and Fort Mitchell that his sons Jerry and Robert "Spike" took over, respectively.

In 1962, Mike passed away, and his sons, Bill and Jim, moved the business to Lookout Heights at Sleepy Hollow and Amsterdam Roads. They bought the store from the Yoder family, who operated a grocery there. A block away on Altavia, many of the Finke clan had already moved from the city, because the Covington streetcar ran by the end of the street. At one time, more than six Finke families had houses on Altavia, each with their own smokehouse in the back.

Bill would buy out his brother, Jim, who went on to work in other Greater Cincinnati meat businesses. That meant the business would pass on to Bill's sons, Don, Tim and Billy Jr., the latter who now makes the goetta. Little did he know that as his business expanded, it would become a landmark stop for northern Kentuckians headed to Fort Wright or Park Hills. Bill Sr. expanded the store when he closed the liquor store, which he operated next door, and also added a back stockroom.

Today, Finke's is humming with customers any time of the day. In the afternoon, the meat counter is busy with customers coming by on their lunch hour for a sandwich. There's an evening rush as people stop by to pick up meat for dinner.

Finke buys all his sides of beef from New Horizon Meats in Cincinnati, which sells to only a dozen or so customers locally. It's fresher than the pre-cut, boxed beef that the larger retailers use, which comes from slaughterhouses out West. And that's Finke's focus: superior quality and service to their customers. You can taste it in their goetta, meatballs and pork sausage, all made on-site.

GOURMET BRAND GOETTA—THE OTHER FINKE GOETTA

Another brother of Mike's, Gene Finke, started out as a brakeman for the Louisville and Nashville Railroad, but a layoff during the Depression sent him into the meat delivery business for the H.H. Meyer Company in Fort Wright and Park Hills, delivering their products to customers in Fort Wright and Park Hills.

Then the 1937 flood sent him to buy a house on Altivia, where his other Finke relatives had settled. He expanded the business, using the former backyard horse stable as a smokehouse to cure hams and make sausages, which he sold on his route and to the restaurants that lined Dixie Highway from Covington to Florence. He would later add goetta to his repoitore, which he made for his brothers' meat delivery routes and for cousins Bill and Jim at the Amsterdam Road store. Some of the other brothers sold his hams and sausages as well.

Gene's son Ray took over his father's Fort Wright and Park Hills truck route after returning from service in World War II. His other son, Dick, bought his ham, sausage and goetta business in 1965. In 1967, Dick replaced the old horse stable with a refrigerated plant and smokeroom to support his one-thousand-hams-a-year business. His sons Paul and Jeffery helped out until going off to college, when their sisters took over helping their father. It was a good time to update the plant, because, in the early 1970s, meat inspection changed from the state to a more strict, federal inspection plan. As the smokehouse and plant were in a residential neighborhood, it was grandfathered into the new federal regulations, but things continued to get tougher for the business.

During that time, Gene still made goetta at his house next door to Dick for the Amsterdam Finke Brothers store of Bill and Jim, and for his son Ray, his uncle Spike and for select restaurant customers. It served as a nice "hobby business" for Gene in his retirement. His wife, Gertrude, still sewed the muslin bags into which the goetta and sausages were stuffed.

In the 1990s, a challenging market forced Dick into focusing on goetta rather than sausage. His father had stopped making goetta, and Bill Finke had started making his own goetta after expanding the store at Sleepy Hollow. Restaurants along Dixie were closing, and retail chains popped up that were not familiar with the old local Germanic meat products like goetta. Dick had landed a few LaRosa's chain accounts with his pork sausage, but it wasn't on Buddy LaRosa's approved sausage list, and that business died down.

So Dick embarked on a seven-year journey to perfect the recipe that he would sell as Dick Finke's All Meat Goetta. Getting his pinhead oats in bulk from Fedder's Feed & Seed in Covington and making the goetta in his backyard smokehouse in one-hundred-pound batches, Dick sold to customers like the Amos Shinkle House Bed & Breakfast, Remke Markets, McHales Meats and Deli in Erlanger and Herringer's Meats in Covington.

Dick's tested goetta recipe would become the Gourmet Brand Goetta that is now made by his son, Jeffery Finke, great-great-grandson of the founder, George Finke Sr. I had the wonderful opportunity to have a goetta dinner with Jeffery and his wife in their northern Kentucky home. Although I didn't get the secret recipe, I do know that they crisp the dish for four minutes on each side at medium heat for the perfect crispiness. Their Gourmet Brand Goetta is a more traditional, older version of goetta, like my grandmother's, with coarsely chopped onions that you can see in the patty and chunks of meat, with a coarser chop than most goettas. It has a great texture and a good bite; it crisps nicely and has a good beef flavor. You can find it locally at summer festivals like the St. Joseph Academy Pigfest in Walton, Kentucky, and the St. Anthony Church Summer Festival in Taylor Mill, Kentucky, and hopefully soon in local retail stores.

I offer a big goetta salute to all the Finke family goetta makers over the past 140 years: George Sr., Louise, Mike, Gene, Dick, Jeffrey, Jim and Billy Jr. There is certainly no other family in greater Cincinnati or northern Kentucky that has a legacy of so many overworked forearms!

Chapter 4

QUEEN CITY SAUSAGE

There's nothing discreet about the Queen City Sausage campus on Spring Grove Avenue and Straight Street. A rampant flying pig sculpture from the Cincinnati Big Pig Gig graces the roof of the front building, erected in 1888. It's a monument, really, to this area—the historic meatpacking district along Camp Washington's Spring Grove Avenue—that gave Cincinnati its "Porkopolis" nickname in the 1880s. Big names like Kahns and many others had slaughterhouses and production facilities here. Now, they're all gone, and Queen City Sausage is the last one standing.

Cincinnati's spry eighty-eight-year-old Sausage King, Elmer Hensler, has reigned over his sausage empire here since his founding of the company in 1965. With only $13,000 in starting capital, he turned Queen City into a multimillion-dollar enterprise. And he has a framed list of forty Cincinnati meat companies that have folded since he started. Elmer is truly a walking history museum, having worked in the industry since he was eleven and forgetting more about all the local meatpacking companies in Cincinnati than most of us will ever know. I came here to meet Elmer and his employees as part of this big goetta project, because he's the largest goetta producer in Cincinnati. If anyone knows about goetta and its origins, it's him. This campus has expanded more than twelve times and is a merging of several facilities, including an old foundry and several old sausage makers. He plans to create more refrigeration areas inside and has enough room in the back of the complex to expand even more. Investing in new equipment is not something Elmer is afraid to do to make the best-quality sausages and goetta Cincinnati has to offer.

Although the company has always made goetta, it's only been since it hired marketing director Mark Balasa eight years ago that its production of the local delicacy has amped up to the level it is today. Mark is the mastermind behind Goettafest and spent twelve years working for Glier's in Covington. He brings a guerrilla marketing approach to goetta and Queen City Sausage's other brands. With Mark's help, in 2011, the Queen City Sausage goetta recipe was tweaked and improved to its current deliciousness. The team felt it needed a few minor improvements. This improved goetta was promoted with a billboard campaign throughout Cincinnati. Have goetta's cousins, scrapple and livermush, ever had their own billboard? I think not.

Elmer Hensler, owner of Queen City Sausage, holding his goetta inside the factory. *Author's collection.*

This improved recipe uses four secret spices. Queen City Sausage's goetta has a good onion flavor and a deeper spice flavor than most other goettas on the market. Its meats and onions are ground fairly fine, and it crisps up nice in a pan. They say it's about 60 percent less fat than the competitive product yet delivers the full goetta taste. It's also 50 percent less fat than traditional breakfast sausage.

On the company's website, it promotes goetta as a great slider, a key component to a good Reuben and part of a goetta grilled cheese.

For a company more than fifty years old, its approaches are not outdated. It has a large social media footprint and several key local brand sponsorships. Elmer is a storyteller, and the company website promotes his storytelling of early days in Cincinnati's meat industry.

Queen City Sausage has been the official bratwurst of the Cincinnati Reds since 2010 and has expanded that sponsorhip to include being the official mettwurst of the team. In a long tradition of German fussball or soccer clubs, whose stadiums each have a house sausage, which they call their "stadionwurst," Queen City is the official sausage of the FC Cincinnati soccer team. One FC Cincy fan said on social media, "If I could get a Hofbrau beer and a Queen City Sausage on rye with sauerkraut, I may never leave the stadium. I could live there." I'd say the same thing about their goetta.

When it comes to goetta, Mark says the easiest way to describe and market it to anyone not familiar with the dish is to say it's a breakfast meat made from pinhead oats, beef, pork, onions and spices. That way, they can identify it with a meal and then start understanding it. Only us Cincinnatians understand the complex history and background of goetta that connects us to our immigrant past.

In addition to goetta, Queen City makes a variety of sausages—andouille, Italian, chorizo—including local Cincinnati brats and metts. Elmer says their metts are basically Hamilton metts without the mustard seed. They make a long list of lunch meats, including Leona, Dutch and Pepper loafs, as well as headcheese and souse, known locally by old German Cincinnatians as schwartenmagen and sutze. They have a bierwurst made with local Hudepohl 14 K, and there's a potential there might be a Rhinegeist beer sausage in the future. The two companies are about to become neighbors, as Rhinegeist is expanding brewing operations to a large complex down the street from Queen City Sausage.

The day of my visit, I pass a two-story image of the Sausage Queen logo as I ascend the outside steps to the second-story offices, the brain trust of this remarkable meat factory. Inside the lobby, I look through a glass window and see Elmer signing checks for his employees; many of whom I will meet have worked over thirty years for him. One worker, George, helped his son pay for his schooling to earn a master's in education. That son, Ken Blackwell, would become mayor of Cincinnati. Elmer looks up, smiles and buzzes me into the brain trust.

The Queen logo of Queen City Sausage. *Author's collection.*

While Elmer finishes up I am led to the conference room, which is where he'll host a lunch for me during which he'll showcase their products, which he graciously does for all visitors. The walls are filled floor to ceiling with old photos, articles and posters of the history of the company and Cincinnati's Porkopolis past. I even get a peek at some of the promotional materials for its Wicked Sausage line, a family of six hot pepper sausages Queen City released with Jungle Jim's, Findlay Market and other local retailers this year.

Elmer grew up in Cincinnati's West End, another faded piece of our past. After surviving the 1937 flood at a home on Gest Street and Freeman Avenue, his mother, Nora, found a house on York Street owned by the Procters of Procter & Gamble, where Elmer grew up. His father, Milton, was a switchman for the railroads, and with eight siblings, Elmer knew any fortune he made would have to be earned. At eleven, he started hanging around the stockyards, helping out in the early mornings before school. He has a great story about one of the teachers swatting him so hard he fell out a window as he was saying hello to some girls at the school across the street. Soon, he would be working on the slaughtering floors, stirring blood from the meat to make beutelwurst or Johnny-in-the-Bag blood sausages for one of his first employers. Because Queen City doesn't slaughter, it has never made a blood sausage.

Elmer's first business partner was a German immigrant from Munich, Alois Stadler, who had worked locally for Karl Frank and Edelmann's. They later brought in George Nadel, a Yugoslavian immigrant master sausage maker who had worked for Roland Meats. Elmer bought both of them out in 2001.

Queen City Goetta comes in one-pound tubes, premium five-pound bricks for the larger commercial customers and the new, individually vacuum-packed EZ Open Goetta Slices. I think the individual slices is a brilliant way to package goetta, and Queen City is the only one doing it. Now you can cook individual slices without having to worry about keeping the rest of the tube fresh until the next cooking. Each package comes with twelve individual slices, which can be peeled open at any of the four corners of each slice. Seasonally, Queen City also makes a link goetta that harkens back to the old oatmeal rings that many local butchers used to make for customers who liked their goetta in link form rather than slab form. This is similar to how pinkel, a goetta ancestor, is served in the area around Hanover and Oldenburg in Germany's Goetta Cradle.

Kroger is the company's largest goetta and sausage customer, but Elmer is proud to supply restaurants, like his friend Johnny Johnson's Camp Washington Chili, another Cincinnati icon just up the street in Camp Washington. Johnny Johnson and Elmer are about the same age. Johnny had recently emigrated from Greece to work at the chili parlor for his uncle Steve Andon back in the early forties, when both were in their early teens. Elmer would come into the restaurant while skipping school. If a truant officer was near, John let Elmer hide under a table until the coast

Newly packaged goetta in the factory of Queen City Sausage. *Author's collection.*

The Queen City Sausage EZ Pack Goetta label. *Courtesy of Queen City Sausage.*

was clear. Today, over seventy years later, the two are great buddies, but now Elmer remains in his seat the entire meal!

Another big restaurant customer of Queen City's goetta is Matt Grimes, owner of the Colonial Cottage in northern Kentucky. No restaurant in the state of Kentucky serves more goetta than Colonial Cottage. They serve it golden-fried and delicious, as a breakfast side, integrated into other dishes like their goetta nachos and their goetta stuffing at Thanksgiving.

Several new dishes have been invented by other enterprising restaurateurs with Queen City Goetta. Chloe's Eatery has developed a dish called Goetta Tots. And the Fry Box at Great American Ballpark opened the 2018 baseball season with a goetta gravy–topped goetta tot. Maybe Queen City will become the first official goetta of the Reds. A family restaurant called the Sunnyside Grill in Cleves, Ohio, makes a dish it calls the Smelvin, which might be called a Cincinnati version of the Rochester, New York Garbage Plate. The Smelvin is a cardio-blasting pile of eggs, goetta, bacon and American cheese on top of home fries and drizzled in gravy. Comfort food, beware of the goetta invasion!

None of Queen City's products is ever frozen, and only good-quality meats—no fillers—are added. Certainly, there is no mechanically separated chicken present, which most national producers use in their hot dogs and sausages.

Matt Grimes, the owner of Colonial Cottage, the largest user of goetta in greater Cincinnati. *Courtesy of Queen City Sausage.*

After a history of the business from Elmer, we take a plant tour. Our tour starts with the cutting area, where the Cottage Ham is taken out of the cut known as the Boston Butt, which is actually the pork shoulder. They let me take pictures of the plant and are completely transparent about their procedures. They should—they have nothing to hide, as quality is king at Queen City Sausage. I'm amazed at how clean and bright the plant is. It's like a Willy Wonka factory of pork bliss, and I am as excited as Charlie Bucket. It's highly automated but still monitored closely by employees. I almost expect the workers, donned in bleached white hoodies as insulation from the refrigeration, to break into an Oompa Loompa song about goetta and sausages. Each area has its own wonderful, distinct smell as we progress through the meat-grinding, filling, smoking and packaging rooms. Unlike others, who use liquid smoke, Queen City uses real hickory wood to smoke its metts and other products.

We pass the smoking and steaming chambers on the tour. Cincinnati brats are steamed, not smoked like the metts. You're tempted to taste one of the cooling sausages off the hanging tree after it comes from the smoker. But I'm not going to do anything to get ejected from this amazing plant tour. No stealing of an Everlasting Gobstopper like the bad kids in Willy Wonka's plant. I mention to Elmer that I'm more of a brat man than a mett man. So he pulls a brat off of a tree that has just exited the steaming chamber and says, "Here, taste a brat that has not yet seen human hands." It's wonderful. It has a smooth texture, enabled by their $300,000 boss mixer that handles all their fine-grind sausages. You can taste the pork and the fresh parsley and seasonings.

We pass pallets of pinhead oats, or oat groats, as they're known anywhere outside of Cincinnati. They come in fifty-pound bags from Richardson Mills. The oats, which will go into the goetta, come from Canada. (Thankfully, President Donald Trump's tariffs have not extended to oats. What an uproar there would be in Cincinnati if tariffs on pinhead oats increased the store price of goetta!)

Elmer takes me into the spice room, where all the spices for Queen City's goetta and sausages are mixed and staged. They don't buy pre-blended spices like most other competitors. They take the extra steps and blend fresh spices themselves. This is the domain of Elmer's younger brother Art, who who is eighty-six. Art retired from his first career, and his brother asked if he would join him making sausages. He's a shorter, slim man with the cheerful disposition of a Keebler elf, and he is the master of flavor for Queen City. Art lets me smell the goetta spices he's mixed, which are wonderful. I get a peak at the spice book that holds all the secret formulas for their products. I'll never tell! Art then shows me the small stand mixer he was using to mix spices in the past. He said to Elmer, "You're killing me with this small mixer!" So, for Art's eightieth birthday, Elmer bought him a horizontal mixer that has about four times the mixing capacity as the original one. If I am as spry and passionate as these two men when I'm in my late eighties, I should be so lucky.

Queen City makes about five thousand pounds of goetta per day. In 2015, Queen City Sausage released a linked version of goetta they call the Goetta Dawg. It's a fully cooked, linked goetta sausage reminiscent of the old Cincinnati local butchers' oatmeal rings of the past. It's great on the grill and even in coneys.

When asked about where goetta may have been first introduced locally, Elmer says he thinks it may have come from Cincinnati's West Side. He said butchers from the West Side would come to him to buy his pork butts to make their own goetta.

We end the day with lunch in the conference room. It's Skyline coneys with Queen City andouille sausage and a special treat: chip wheelie ice

Elmer Hensler and artists Matt Lynch and Curtis Goldstein in front of the Queen City Sausage Mural. *Courtesy of Queen City Sausage.*

cream sandwiches from Graeter's. Elmer says it always helps to make friends with other Cincinnati food companies. We talk about the history of goetta and what's facing the meat industry today. Then, I thank Elmer, Mark and the operations guys for my tour and their hospitality, knowing that I just had an amazing, rare glimpse into Cincinnati's Porkopolis legacy.

To honor its legacy, Queen City was included as part of a local art project called Work/Surface, a series of Formica mosaics. The project is inspired by the "Worker Murals" created by German American artist Winold Reiss for the Cincinnati Union Terminal opening in 1933. University of Cincinnati art professor Matt Lynch and Columbus, Ohio artist Curtis Goldstein collaborated to produce a suite of laser-cut Formica, high-pressure, laminate, mosaic murals of current Cincinnati industries. Like the original Reiss tile mosaics, which included Kahn's Meats to represent our strong meatpacking industry, the two artists included a scene inside the Queen City factory to represent what's left of that industry now. This mural now has a permanent home in the Cincinnati Art Museum, on the ground floor near the DeWitt entrance.

Elmer has no plans for retirement. And the demand for Queen City's goetta doesn't seem to be peaking or plateauing. In January 2019,

Elmer hosted the first Queen City Goettafest in Naples, Florida, at Michelbob's Championship Ribs, sponosored by 700 WLW Radio. This was the first goetta festival of any kind outside of the greater Cincinnati area. While Naples has a lot of Cincinnati snowbirds, the locals had an introduction to our beloved peasant food. Cincinnati is very lucky to have a hometown goetta producer who puts so much effort into quality and innovation.

Chapter 5

GLIER'S

FROM VIOLINS TO GOETTA

The factory on Goetta Way in Covington, Kentucky, where Glier's Meats, the largest goetta producer in the world, operates, seems out of a German fairy tale. The old building was erected by the Bavarian Brewery in the 1880s to make Riedlin Select Beer, named after Wilhelm Riedlin, the German immigrant founder of the brewery. Situated just north of the Mainstrasse and Mutter Gottes German neighborhoods of Covington, the factory resembles a German castle. It's down the street from the oldest surviving Covington Turnhalle in greater Cincinnati, a German sport and social club, where Riedlin served as president, and across from one of the most famous taverns that serves goetta, twenty-four hours a day, the Anchor Grill.

Dan Glier, the current owner and president, is son of the founder, Robert "Bob" Glier, who started the company in 1946. Glier's is proud of its history—both the family history and the legacy immigrant product it crafts in hand-stirred, 180-pound batches daily. That's about the largest batch a human can physically stir. You can tell who stirs goetta at the factory by the size of their forearms. Look out, Crossfitters—this may be the next new exercise. Three-foot-long canoe-like paddles are the implements that evenly distribute the pork and beef throughout the oat mixture. About thirty employees support the goetta operation at Glier's, many of whom have worked there several decades.

Glier's standard goetta, which accounts for 90 percent of its sales, is a pork and beef product that includes pork hearts and skins and contains 50

Above: The Glier's goetta factory was originally a bottling plant for Bavarian's Riedlin Select Beer, as shown here. *Courtesy of Glier's.*

Right: All Glier's goetta is ground and hand-stirred, as shown here. *Courtesy of Kenton County Public Library.*

percent meat, as well as pinhead oats and Spanish onions. When Dorsel was still a local company, Glier's used to buy its leftover oats after Labor Day to help it out. Now, Glier's buys so much, it buys direct from Richardson Mills. It's Glier's recipe, consistency and flavor that many greater Cincinnatians associate with goetta.

Glier's is probably the most visible brand of goetta in Kroger and other greater Cincinnati retail grocers, although Queen City Sausage is its biggest and most formidable competitor. Glier's also provides goetta to the largest number of restaurants in the area, like Frisch's, Price Hill Chili and many others. Glier's has also done a lot to support the survival of goetta in greater Cincinnati. It sponsors the annual Goettafest in Newport, Kentucky, and, more recently, has sponsored weekly parties on the Purple People Bridge during the warmer weather months. The company has made goetta accessible to the masses in grills, stovetops and microwaves. It has also dispelled the myths of mystery meat through education and change in its original pronunciation, from "gudda" to "gedda."

Although it's the Glier family crest that adorns Glier's goetta packaging, it's not the Glier male line that the goetta recipe comes through. The Gliers are descended from fourteen generations of *geigenbauer* ("violin makers"), dating back to Johann Gottlieb Glier in 1632. They came from Klingenthal, in the famous Markneunkirchen region of Germany, known as the "Corner of Music" due to its high production of musical instruments. There was nothing further from their minds than butchery. Robert C. Glier (1848–1927), grandfather of the founder, immigrated to Cincinnati in 1870 after serving in the Franco-Prussian War. He worked for Rudolph Wurlitzer Company from 1883 to 1900 before opening his own violin shop, where in his long career he made over four thousand violins in the style of Italian Stradivarius. From his Fourth and Sycamore shop, Glier became known as one of the finest violin makers in America. His son Robert Jr. took over the shop after his father's death in 1927, but the *Cincinnati Post* said this about the third generation in 1927, "The survival of the Glier tradition rests on two boys, the sons of the present Glier. The older boy, 20, (Bill), does not seem to take to the art, Glier says. Time alone can tell what the younger (Bob) will do." And time told that he would start the world's largest goetta factory.

So it's through the founders' maternal line of Emma Yung Glier that we find the goetta tradition. Emma's grandfather was Johann Peter Yung, who had immigrated from Horingen, Germany, in the Rhineland. Johann Peter and his wife, Catherine Roux, had settled in a small German Lutheran immigrant farm community called Hayfield about five miles south of

Alexandria, Kentucky. Johann Peter's sons would have been very familiar with animal butchery on the farm. By the 1920s, however, J.P.'s son Peter, Emma's father, had decided he'd had enough of farm life and moved to the bustling city of Newport, Kentucky, and established his own butcher shop. His sons Frank and Peter would learn from their father and establish their own butcher shops.

Neither Bob Glier nor his brother Bill had any interest in making violins. Bob had started working in 1925 at his Uncle Peter Yung's butcher shop on Monmouth Street in Newport after school. Here, he learned the trade and the ingredients of the Yung family goetta.

Bob Glier didn't like the porridge-like goetta of his mother but loved the rest of her cooking. The goetta she and her family made was thinner, had less meat and was stored in crocks with a layer of congealed fat on the top during the colder winter months. Emma Glier had been a pastry chef at the Colonnade Restaurant for eight years, famous for her yeast donuts and lemon meringue pie. She would later say that when she made goetta for her son, she had to use his recipe.

From 1938 to 1942, Bob worked at the large H.H. Meyer Packing Company in Cincinnati, Ohio, which would become Partridge Meats. It was here that Bob started formulating his own goetta recipe. He told the *Cincinnati Enquirer* in 1968: "I decided to come up with something of my own because I didn't like my mother's goetta. She prepared a kind of German oatmeal with ground pork that was just too soft and sloppy for me. It was like eating grits." Although he came up with a successful formula that now supplies over two hundred outlets in Kentucky alone and churns out thousands of pounds of goetta daily, he was mystified by the origin of the dish.

Originally hired as a kitchen helper, his interest in sausage-making got him the coveted apprentice to the master sausage maker. Also during that time, his brother Bill Glier became owner of Peter Yung & Company Meats, because their Uncle Pete Yung's daughter was not interested in taking over the butchery. Bill would operate it until 1969, when it merged with Glier's Meats.

Bob served in the U.S. Army Air Corps from 1942 to 1946. During that time, he sent money home to his mother, Emma Yung Glier. But his recently widowed mother already had a job and didn't need the money, so she saved it for him. When he came home from the war, Emma gave him the seed money that allowed him to buy a small retail butchery with a small sausage kitchen at 439 Pike Street in Covington. Here, he began making his own sausages and goetta.

Bob Glier stirring goetta in the Glier's factory. *Courtesy of Public Library of Cincinnati and Hamilton County.*

By the late 1950s, Bob had seen the immense potential in providing just goetta. In 1964, he bought an old dairy building on Gordon Street in Cincinnati and opened a second "Goetta Factory" with the intent to distribute products in Ohio under state inspection. Stands like Russ Gibbs in the Findlay Market began to sample and sell Glier's goetta. Then, with the passage of the Wholesome Meat Act in 1967, which required federal inspection of meat plants, Bob bought the current factory at Goetta Way and consolidated both operations there.

From the 1960s to the 1980s, Glier's was branded as "Gliers' Good Goetta." Its brand mascot was a cute pig in a chef's hat and checkered apron. A 1964 advertising campaign in the *Cincinnati Post* vigorously promoted Glier's goetta, as the company desired to open up a larger market. It promoted its goetta as old-fashioned, truly homemade and with a high meat content, calling it "The Meaty Kind" It also incorrectly connected it to the Rhineland area of Germany, near where Bob Glier's mother's family hailed from. The description was straight out of a *Mad Men* episode: "Protein packed with juicy chunks of lean beef and pork, just the right amount of hearty, rib

A Glier's advertisement from the 1950s. *Courtesy of Public Library of Cincinnati and Hamilton County.*

sticking oatmeal, and a combination of zesty, old world seasonings right out of a generations old recipe." Another Glier's ad proclaimed goetta as "a delicious man-pleasing cold weather dish that only takes minutes to prepare."

Glier's was the first company to introduce goetta in packages that held up on shelves. In 1965, they worked with TeePac, a large national packaging company, to develop a double-wound saran package. It could be printed on the middle layer, filled with hot product and would hold up tight and shrink when the product cooled. Having a package accept the product hot during packaging ensured greater food safety and a longer shelf life, as well as better distribution options. This made what was a September–May "goetta season" a year-round proposition. And so goetta production at Glier's increased. Vaccuum packing equipment from Kryovac became available and allowed Glier's to package larger blocks of goetta, which are sold to institutions and large users. Walmart gets an exclusive two-pound tube to sell. We can thank Glier's and its packaging innovation in popularizing goetta as an all-year product in the greater Cincinnati area. But it hadn't made it from the breakfast table to the grill, as it would in later years with more innovative Glier's products.

Meeting Breakfast Resistance?

TRY GLIER'S GOOD GOETTA

Gets the whole family off to a rousing good start!

Masterful breakfasts call for a really substantial tempting dish—and that's the time for you to call on GLIER'S GOOD GOETTA! It's an old-fashioned, truly homemade style goetta that's meatier than most . . . protein-packed with juicy chunks of lean beef and pork, just the right amount of hearty, rib-sticking oatmeal and a combination of zesty, old-world seasonings right out of a generations-old recipe. Makes family breakfast easier for the lady of the house because it takes just minutes to prepare . . . and dad and the kids will love its pipin'-hot goodness these nippy mornings. Try it now . . . costs just pennies-per-portion!

GLIER'S GOOD GOETTA

DISTRIBUTED BY L. J. BUEGEL DIST. CO.

1700 Blue Rock St., Cincinnati, Ohio   Phone 681-4

Left: Another Glier's advertisement from the 1950s. *Courtesy of the Public Library of Cincinnati and Hamilton County.*

Below: Dan Glier (*center*) labelling roll goetta in the plant. *Courtesy of Glier's.*

Send them a gift from home.

Glier's good goetta in a holiday gift pack.

Cincinnati expats have long requested goetta to be sent all over the world. *Courtesy of Public Library of Cincinnati and Hamilton County.*

In the late 1960s, Bob brought tamales into the goetta plant, mixing the cornmeal in the same vats in which they mixed the pinhead oatmeal, but that didn't last long. Very few items that took the company's focus away from goetta made it to their current lineup of products. Glier's also makes a line of Oktoberfest sausages, which are the official line of the Cincinnati Bengals, and a line of deli meats.

In 1972, after graduating from Eastern Kentucky University, Bob's son Dan Glier entered the business full time, taking over as president in 1977. He continues to run the business today. Dan's leadership has allowed the company to evolve and bring new goetta products to market.

After many customer requests, in 1988, Glier's added more spices and red pepper to its formula to create Hot Goetta. In 1997, to address customer demand, the company introduced a lower-fat turkey version, and many of the local butchers followed. In the same way the pressure cooker, and then the Crock-Pot, affected the formulation of goetta,

A Glier's factory worker wrapping roll goetta. *Courtesy of Kenton County Public Library.*

Americans' need for quick-prep convenience foods has made Glier's develop new forms of goetta suitable for microwave and grill. To promote goetta as more than just a breakfast food, Glier's introduced two new products in 2000, designed to be easily prepared on the grill without falling apart as the traditional slabs had done, or even microwaved. Thus were born Goetta Bun Links, or Goetta Dogs, and Goetta Sandwich slices, or Goetta Burgers.

A bacon goetta was introduced in 2015. The idea came about through David Glier, third generation of the Glier family, and his group of friends. It debuted at the Bacon Bourbon and Brew Festival in Newport, Kentucky.

As with any good company, some products need to be retired. The all-beef goetta was one of those products. It goes to show that in Porkopolis, you simply must have pork in your goetta.

The recent "Goetta Anytime" campaign continues to promote goetta for any meal with even more new products. The recent obsession with sliders

Right: Former Bengal Ken Anderson promotes Glier's sliders. *Courtesy of Glier's.*

Below: The goetta sliders kit. *Author's collection.*

In 2006, Glier's produced this recipe and history book to promote its goetta products. *Author's collection.*

and casual party foods motivated the new Goetta Sliders kit, which includes sweet Hawaiian buns and dill pickles, and the goetta bites product, which includes cayenne and bits of cheddar cheese. Although Glier's doesn't recommend any certain way to eat your goetta, it is a maple syrup–dressed or plain-dressed family. You'll find no ketchup at a Glier family breakfast.

The Glier's product is getting stronger in central Kentucky—the Louisville, Lexington, Bowling Green and Somerset markets. The challenge is getting a critical mass to distribute it. Dan Glier echoes what others, like Queen City Sausage, say: "Dayton, Ohio just doesn't get goetta!" They can't seem to get a foothold there, even though they are expanding in Columbus.

Another thing that Glier's has been smart about is merchandising. The company created Mr. Goetta, a plush character in the shape of a one-pound goetta tube that walks around at events to promote the brand. Greater Cincinnatians can buy hats, T-shirts, mugs, stickers, magnets and the like to show their Glier's pride.

THE COVINGTON JEWELER WHO CHANGED THE PRONUNCIATION OF *GOETTA*

In Cincinnati, you know how long goetta has been a part of a family's tradition by how they pronounce it. Both of my grandmothers pronounced it as it was originally pronounced, "gudda." Up to about the mid-1950s, in both the *Cincinnati Enquirer* and the *Post*, it was sometimes spelled "guetta" in articles. That was just how many greater Cincinnatians pronounced it at the time. But Glier's would change all that, to take a big stigma away.

Dan Glier thought that pronouncing it "gutta" connected it to guts, or organs and scraps—what many people thought were included in this mysterious grain sausage. He noticed that there was a jewelry and watch company in Covington called Goetz, shared the same umlauted "o" as in goetta. That business had been in the Covington business district a long time, in an old building at the corner of Pike and Madison. So, using Goetz as an example, Dan Americanized the umlauted *o* and began his campaign of pronouncing it the way that is the more accepted pronunciation today: "getta."

Chapter 6

JOHANN CHRISTIAN DORSEL

THE ORIGINAL MR. PINHEAD

Until recently, it was easy to find Dottie Dorsel's Self-Rising Flour and Cornmeal on the shelves in the baking aisle at any Kroger grocery in greater Cincinnati. Dorsel's is surrounded by other brand mascots, like the Pillsbury Doughboy, Aunt Jemima and Robin Hood. Sure, each of these well-known national brands has its own competing cornmeals and flours. But Dottie has something they don't have: pinhead oatmeal, the key ingredient in goetta.

In the late 1700s, the English writer and philosopher Samuel Johnson snarkily lampooned the Scottish oats eater, saying, "Oats are a grain that in England are generally fed to horses, while in Scotland, support the people." The Scottish writer James Boswell replied, "Aye that's why in England there are fine horses, and in Scotland, fine people." The Scottish even include oats in their national grain sausage, haggis. Germans, too, have long known the health benefits of oatmeal and, for that matter, other stewed grains.

Horses, brewers, bakers and greater Cincinnatians have long known the nutritional value of pinhead oats. Goetta is just not goetta without the pinhead oats. Regular, rolled oats make goetta too mushy. Pinhead oats have more body and impart a nuttier taste. Steel cut oats are basically whole oat groats cut up into smaller pieces by a steel blade, somewhat resembling chopped-up rice. Because these oats aren't processed by steaming or rolling, they take longer to cook than rolled oats, thus having a chewier, nuttier and more toothsome texture.

The advantage of eating pinhead oats is that they impart a feeling of fullness, keeping you energized for longer. This is because these oats are thicker and less processed, thus slowing digestion. Slower digestion means a lower glycemic index value, which can help prevent diabetes and benefit those with diabetes as it slows down the rate sugar is introduced into your body.

So it's no surprise that the popularity of our beloved dish within the German community in northern Kentucky and greater Cincinnati spawned a retail supplier of pinhead oats. Immigrants from the northern farm regions of Germany were already familiar with nonrolled or milled oats, which were known in English as oat groats. While commercial-sized fifty- and one-hundred-pound bags of steel cut oats—the more common name of pinhead oats—are available to institutions, Dorsel's has brought consumer-sized two-pound portions to home goetta makers for over half a century. And we have a German immigrant from goetta country, the original Mr. Pinhead himself, Johann Christian Dorsel, to thank for this. And, if it weren't for an accidental default on a mortgage that Mr. Pinhead took over, we may never have had a retail pinhead oat, and goetta may have faded into obscurity.

You have to be careful today with the term *steel cut oats*. Quaker and some other brands market a "steel cut instant oats product." But that's a contradiction in terms. You can't have instant oats if the oat is unrolled and whole, without the husk. It just takes longer to cook real pinhead oats. Apparently, there is no distinction any more that *steel cut* refers to groats or pinhead oats, and these companies claiming steel cut oats are taking big liberties on the term. More and more steel cut oats brands are popping up, like Bob's Redmill and John McCann's Steel Cut Irish Oatmeal. For the Cincinnati ex-pat goetta maker, these brands are suitable replacements for Dottie Dorsel's. Bob's Redmill has even gotten into the goetta game, posting a recipe for goetta on its website, but incorrectly saying, "It's nearly identical to what the Pennsylvania Dutch call scrapple."

Johann Christian Dorsel, founder of the Dorsel Flour Company. *Courtesy of Kenton County Public Library.*

The original Dottie Dorsel logo (*left*) and the current logo (*right*). *Author's collection.*

The brand mascot, Dottie Dorsel's persona, has changed quite a bit since she was created in the late 1950s by the third-generation owner of the company, Norbert J. Dorsel. Now, she looks like a racially neutral but mildy African American female chef. Originally, Dottie was a happy-go-lucky housewife with yellow chef's hat, brunette bobbed hair and a toothy smile. But Prairie Mills, which has owned the brand since 2006, went the route of Betty Crocker and updated her image to appeal to a more universal audience.

In 2009, when updating from the old kraft paper package to a new resealable poly stand-up pouch, Gary Swaim, national sales manager for Prairie Mills, also decided to give Dottie a facelift. The company thought the old Dottie had sort of a "Suzy Homemaker" image, and they knew that the American woman had gone through quite a change since the 1950s. While they wanted to maintain a link with the past, they also wanted to give Dottie the feel of a modern woman. And so her new look connotes a professional, busy American woman who works outside the home.

Until the 1980s, you could send in your address with ten cents and receive the *Dottie Dorsel Cookbook*, with recipes to use its cornmeal and flour, like Dixie Brownies, and of course its goetta recipe. Although the imaginary Dottie Dorsel is given credit for the goetta recipe on the back of the Dorsel Pinhead Oats package, it was actually the recipe of Amelia Joerg Dorsel, the wife of Fred Dorsel, the founder's son. This recipe is the most common recipe used in greater Cincinnati for home goetta makers and is sort of our version of the Toll House chocolate chip cookie recipe. Although there were several Dottie Dorsels in the line, it's not known if any of them were the namesake of the brand logo. There was Dorothea Dorsel, first child of founder John and his first wife, Elizabeth, and there was Dorothy Wertheimer Dorsel (1907–1992), wife of Paul Dorsel, grandson of the founder.

Dottie Dorsel's Goetta Recipe
1 pound beef
1 pound pork (ground together)
6 cups water
2½ cups Dorsel's Pinhead Oatmeal
1 large onion, sliced
1 to 4 bay leaves (optional)
3 teaspoons salt
A pinch of pepper
Variation (substitute 2 teaspoons dried summer savory in place of onion and bay leaves)

Regular Method
Put water into pan; when boiling, add salt, pepper, and oatmeal. Cook 2 hours, stirring often and keeping lid on while cooking over low heat. Add meat, onion and bay leaves, mix well. Let cook 1 hour, stirring often. Pour into bread pans. When cooked, place in refrigerator. Will keep for days. When ready to use, slice the loaf of goetta and put into a pan in which there is a little hot bacon fat. Fry until well browned.

Slow Cooker Method
Put water, salt and pepper into cooker, cover and heat on high for 20 minutes. Stir in oatmeal, cover and cook on high for 1½ hours. Add meat, onion and bay leaves. Mix well. Cover and cook on low for 3 hours Uncover. If not thick enough, cook a little longer, stirring often. Proceed as in direction No. 5 and No. 6 for regular method.

The interesting thing about this recipe is that it doesn't contain allspice, as most goetta recipes do. It also suggests replacing bay leaf and onion with summer savory, which has piney and peppery notes, but not the flavor of onion. I think that, without onion, goetta would lose much of its traditional flavor. Summer savory can be replaced by sage, thyme and

A family picture of Fred and Amelia Joerg Dorsel, whose recipe is on the Dorsel flour bag. *Courtesy of Kenton County Historical Society.*

marjoram, which are also found in some local recipes. Also, the recipe just notes slicing the onions, not fine-chopping them, or grating them, as many home recipes call for.

I have a family connection to the Dorsels. My maternal grandmother's aunt Loretta Brosey married Jack Dorsel, a grandson of the founder. So you could say that pinhead oats run in my blood. I inherited some furniture that Jack made for my grandmother that I call my "goetta furniture." Jack and Loretta Dorsel had no children, so my grandmother was like a daughter to them. Jack fought with the Fifty-Second Texas Navy in World War I and ended up moving to Dallas to be a salesman for Capital Records.

There's an old family story about Jack Dorsel that was documented in the *Dallas Times Herald* by journalist Warren Bosworth, a witness to the Lee Harvey Oswald shooting, that we call "The Great Sausage Flight of 1952." In 1952, Jack Dorsel, the grandson of the founder of Dorsel Pinhead Oats, was living in Dallas, Texas, with his wife, Loretta Brosey Dorsel. Apparently, Jack complained to his family back home in northern Kentucky about how hard it was to find good German sausages in Texas and that he couldn't find any as good as the ones in Cincinnati.

So Jack's favorite nephew, William, and his wife packed up two suitcases full of sausages—eight pounds of Cincinnati metts, five pounds of Cincinnati brats and three five-pound Johnny-in-the-Bag sausages. They boarded a flight with nothing else and presented this sausage hoard to their beloved uncle so he'd stop his complaining. Now that's love! It was such a big deal, the Dallas newspaper photographed Uncle Jack, nephew William and William's wife with their sausages, documenting this local delicacy. The sausage mentioned, Johnny-in-the-Bag, called beutelwurst in Germany, is a close cousin of goetta. It's a grain sausage that uses rye instead of pinhead oats and also has pork blood in it.

The founder of the company, Johann Christian Dorsel, was born the third son of ten children in St. Mauritz bei Munster, Westphalia, Germany, to Johann Bernard Dorsel and Gertrude Marie Koppernagel. This is deep in the heart of Germanic goetta country. Johann's father, John Sr., was an oldest son and owned a large farm, making him a *Kolonus*, a landowner, and thus a very influential community member. Growing up on a farm, J.C. would have been very familiar with the gruetzwurst made from the hog and cattle at the fall slaughter.

In Westphalia, only the oldest son—or oldest daughter, if there were no sons—could inherit the family farm. All other siblings were called *Heurling*, or day laborers, and worked for their oldest sibling. They even had to ask for permission to marry and have children. They were tied to the farm estate into which they were born without any rights or much room for economic growth. They were at the mercy of their oldest sibling's charity and had to accept their position in life or leave for better opportunities. Johann Christian Dorsel's older brother Ignatz would inherit the farm. Johann helped his brother strengthen the farm after the bad management of their father, and after receiving his $150 inheritance from the estate after his father's death, he decided to immigrate to America. He landed in Galveston, Texas, and stayed there less than a year, working as a farmhand. Ignatz Dorsel ended up passing along the Dorsel family farm to his daughter Anna Meckman, along with a prosperous brickmaking business.

John and his large family were members of St. Joseph's Church in Covington, Kentucky. From his first marriage to Elizabeth Kurre, he had nine children, six of whom made it to adulthood: Dora, August, Jospehine, Louisa, Frank and John. And from his second marriage to Mina Staggenborg, who was twenty years younger, he had nine more children, six of whom made it to adulthood: Louise, Fred, Mary, Albert, Nettie and Loretta. J.C. was very active in the Catholic Church and was president of the St. Joseph Orphanage Society from 1878 to 1880. He died in 1922 at the ripe old age of ninety and passed the Dorsel Milling Company to his sons. He served two years as Covington city councilman and was a member of the Covington German Pioneer Association.

For the next nearly forty years after arriving in America, J.C. Dorsel made his fortune in a variety of industries, until his broken road led him to flour milling, grain bartering and pinhead oatmeal manufacturing. After arriving in Covington in 1854, he worked for four years as a coach driver for D.H. Holmes, on whose land would become Holmes High School. He met his wife, who was a maid at the Lavasser House close to the Holmes mansion.

J.C.'s next venture was operating the Dorsel House from 1858 to 1862 on Washington Avenue in Covington. It was a hotel and coffee house. He partnered with his brother-in-law William Middendorf, who had married his sister Louise. William's heavy drinking caused J.C. to remove himself from the partnership and try something else. This heavy drinking also led to the demise of William's next venture—undertaking. However, it was John Dorscl's fortune that led him to build an undertaking business for his widowed sister Louise Middendorf at Pike and Craig Streets in Covington that has grown today into northern Kentucky's largest family-run funeral business.

After this venture, J.C. returned to the familiar—farming—locating a farm in Covington that he turned into a successful dairy farm. He employed two drivers, Frank Wulftange and Herman Dusing, to deliver the milk produced on that farm.

Then, for some reason, he sold his successful dairy business in 1867 to Herman Dusing. He partnered with his other driver, Frank Wulftrange, and built the largest distillery in Kentucky, for rye whiskey, at Twelfth and Rickey Streets in Covington. They operated that business for the next twenty years until a fire destroyed the factory in 1888. That year, J.C. Dorsel bought a large farm, on which he raised and sold chewing tobacco until 1894 under the company name Noonan Dorsel Tobacco Company. During this whole time, Dorsel had been amassing a huge real estate empire in Covington, building and buying houses. He built a huge Italianate mansion in Edgewood, Kentucky, on Duddley Pike.

Sometime while in the distillery business, John C. loaned Herman Hellman, owner of the Newport Flour Mill, $2,500 and took a mortgage out on the mill. The business defaulted on the loan, and J.C. took over the business, renting it to several operators. The first renters were the Hoffman brothers, who relocated the mill to 1106 Monmouth Street. In 1897, the mill was run as the Wehenpohl Mills. J.C. then came out of retirement in 1902 to help run the mills, and by 1907 it had reincorporated as Dorsel Flour Mills. It had been supplying oatmeal from at least 1904.

An image of the original Newport mill that became Dorsel's. *Courtesy of Kenton County Historical Society.*

Fred Dorsel joined his father as the bookkeeper after leaving college and learned the business from top to bottom. He saw the need for some capital improvements and so added a grain elevator and a direct rail line to the mill. As J.C. was aging and unable to really run the business, Fred convinced his brother John to join them. After J.C. and his two sons were all in, they began branding and advertising vigorously. According to son John Jr.: "We started pushing the business hard and advertising and by putting out a high grade of flour, gradually built up a very satisfactory business. We did particularly well during the Great War (WWI), but lost most of the excessive profits made then when the terrific decline in the prices of all commodities occurred in 1921."

That brand was the Seal of Kentucky Flour, with the slogan "Miles of Smiles," made from a mix of Limestone Winter Wheat and Dakota Hard Spring Wheat. One of its largest customers was the Wiedemann Brewery, whose malt house was just across the railroad tracks from the Dorsel Mill. Wiedemann was one of the most popular post-Prohibition beers in greater Cincinnati. An early wood sign advertising Dorsel Seal of Kentucky Flour is on display at the American Sign Museum in Cincinnati.

An original Dorsel Flour sign at the American Sign Museum. *Courtesy of Ted Swormstedt.*

In 1916, an agricultural report gave a description of the Dorsel Milling Company:

> *The Dorsel Company* [Newport, Kentucky], *11th and Monmouth streets* [1106–1108 Monmouth], *operating a 225 bbl flour mill, buys almost 20,000 bbls annually of hard wheat flour for blending. For the last two months the company has run its mill day and night. It is a car buyer of chicken feed, handles self-rising flour made by other mills and is a wholesale grain dealer, buying corn and oats in cars. Fred Dorsel, secretary and treasurer, commenting on wheat, predicted it would reach $22.4 before the next crop—he believes there will be a considerable falling off in the consumption of wheat on account of bakers reducing the size of loaves.*

In 1919, John's fourth son, Albert H. Dorsel, severed ties with the family business and bought the Liberty Mills, owned by the McCoy brothers in Liberty, Indiana. He moved his wife and children to Indiana and incorporated that operation as the Albert H. Dorsel Milling Company, producing the Faultless Flour brand.

> *Newport KY, Albert Dorsel formely connected with the Dorsel Milling Company has purchased the mill at Liberty Indiana, which has been owned by the McCoy brothers. Having purchased the Liberty Mills of McCoy Brothers, I wish to announce to all patrons that it will be my earnest endeavor to give them the highest grade of milling products; fair, just and courteous treatment, and hope to have a continuance of your valued patronage which will be highly appreciated.*

John passed the company on to his son Fred Dorsel after his death in 1922. As the oldest son, Fred had been the bookkeeper for the business since its founding.

> *Cincinnati, Ohio—the Dorsel Grain Co. has been reorganized as a result of the recent death of President John Dorsel. Fred Dorsel has been elected president of the Dorsel Flour Company, and John Dorsel Jr. is now the President of the Dorsel Grain Company, which will move its office from Newport Kentucky to the Swift Building, this city [Cincinnati]. Several years before the founder's death, the Dorsels had established a grain and hay branch. John Jr devoted most of his time to it and enjoyed that business very much.*

The years between the wars saw the horse and buggy make way for the new automobile. Per John Jr.:

> *It was gradually considered then that while the automobile was growing more popular yearly, that horses would be used for short hauls and mills would continue to use wheat and corn. But the auto finally drove out most all the horses and the large flour mills drove out the small ones and Prohibition put the corn grits mills out of business, so the few large grain and hay trades of Cincinnati were almost completely destroyed and put me out of business.*

The split from the milling business and its demise was why John Jr.'s sons never became involved in the business. Then tragedy struck the Dorsel business again. On Sunday, February 14, 1943, the four-story Dorsel Monmouth Street mill was destroyed in a fire totalling $100,000 in damages The shortages of industrial equipment during World War II made it impossible to rebuild the plant. The Dorsels veered their business away from production to distribution. They no longer milled the grains themselves, farming it out to other millers and then packaging and distributing their products. In 1948, they registered the Dorsel brand of products with Wilson Corn Products, a milling company in Rochester, Indiana, to whom they farmed out their milling and to whom they'd later sell the business.

After the death of his father, Fred, in 1946, Norbert Dorsel took over the company. His contribution to the business was moving the company warehouse to Cox Road in Florence, Kentucky, in 1959, near the airport. There was no longer a need to be next to the rail line, and the population

The Dorsel Plant around 1910. *Courtesy of Kenton County Historical Society.*

was moving out to the suburbs along Dixie Highway. Now only packaging and distributing its brands, the company could have moved almost anywhere. The mill property was sold in 1964 to the Camins brothers, who opened a discount furniture store. Although Dorsel had supplied oats since its inception in 1904, it was Norbert who developed the brand persona of Dottie Dorsel and pushed its pinhead oatmeal to retail customers, like Kroger, for the specific purpose of making goetta.

Norbert's son Jerry took over in 1976, operating the company with his second wife, Joan. By the early 1980s, the fifth generation, with Jerry's son Curtis, was set to take the helm when his father retired. By that time, in addition to the Rochester Mill, they were getting the flour and cornmeal from Auburn Rolling Mills in Auburn, Kentucky, and a mill in Kansas. The pinhead oats came from Iowa. Curtis left the company in about 1981. With competition from large national flour companies, Jerry decided to sell the company in 1995 to Wilson Corn Products, which was renamed Prairie Mills after it was acquired in 2006. After the sale, all local packaging ceased, but the Cox Avenue warehouse remained as a distribution center. Prairie Mills is now the exclusive distributor of the Dorsel brand, which it considers a small regional brand.

Just how important Dorsel's pinhead oats are to greater Cincinnatians was revealed during "The Great Pinhead Oats Shortage of 1989." From December 1989 to the end of January 1990, Dorsel's pinhead oats were off the shelves of local groceries. The Dorsel Company, which at that time was getting pinhead oats in four-hundred-pound bags, was put on allottment with its supplier and relegated to one-hundred-pound bags. It couldn't keep up with the demand of home goetta makers. Calls to its facility looking for the oats came in at the rate of ten or more a day. Demand exceeded supply that year, a demand that starts in October and falls off in April, as lighter fare takes center table. But many Christmas and holiday brunches were without homemade goetta throughout the city that fateful year. Even Santa Claus couldn't remedy the situation.

There are two good things about pinhead oats. The first is that they are made from the whole oat kernel before being flatttened or rolled, and second, they are significantly cheaper than more highly processed oats. The only bad thing is that, because they're not processed, they take extra time than processed oats to cook. The lower cost made it an affordable product for the lower- and middle-class German immigrants of northern Kentucky and Cincinnati. Of all the industries Mr. Pinhead dabbled in—dairy, chewing tobacco and whiskey—pinhead oats was the product that would last into the third generation of his offspring. The brand lives on, feeding countless greater Cincinnatians.

Today, almost all pinhead oats come from farms in Canada, including the branded Dorsel Pinhead Oats from the provinces of Alberta, Manitoba and Saskatchewan. A small amount is made in the Northwest United States and the northern central plains of the Dakotas and Nebraska. Larger users like Queen City Sausage buy direct from Richardson Mills, which also supplies oats for Prairie Mills for the Dorsel Brand. North College Hill Bakery buys in bulk and acts, much like Dorsel did, as a local distributor of pinhead oats to local butchers like Hammans, Stehlins and others. Fedder's Feed & Seed in Covington sells pinhead oats from Wisconsin in fifty-pound bags that is used by some butchers in northern Kentucky. Langen Meats buys its pinhead oatmeal in bulk from BakeMark Products in Fairfield.

Richardson Mills, the supplier for the Dorsel brand, is the largest oat miller in North America. Its extensive grain networks allow it to source oats directly from the grower, creating a farm-to-shelf supply chain. Its oat groats are produced by cleaning high-quality raw oats, dehulling and kiln-toasting. Prairie Mills says that the quality of oats is due to good screening of broken groats and foreign objects. Some suppliers are not as good or consistent at the cleaning process as Richardson is. The kilning process protects the groats from rancidity and imparts a toasted flavor while enhancing functionality. The oat groats are then reduced in size

An image of rolled oats (left) and pinhead oats (right). *Author's collection.*

through a process using steel cutting blades, resulting in steel cut oat groats, or what Dorsel's calls pinhead oats.

Steel cut oat groats have grown in popularity as a hot cereal due to the unique cooked texture. Richardson Mills' product development team has created products that shorten cook time while still maintaining a unique texture. Richardson Mills ships its bulk whole oat groats internationally, where they can be processed into flakes in markets that do not grow oats. Their whole and steel cut oat groats are available in bulk (rail and truck), fifty-pound bags and super sacks.

Today, according to Gary Swain, Dorsel's pinhead oatmeal is bought largely by baby boomers. There is still a spike in sales in the colder months and around the holidays, when people come home for Christmas. But people are preparing food less in their homes these days, so there has been a drop in retail sales. Prairie Mills is surprised by the contacts it makes through its website with people who grew up on goetta but live all over the world and are willing to pay freight greater than the cost of the product to have pinhead oats. As a result, the company ships Dorsel pinhead oats from Australia to Austria. While you can still find Dorsel pinhead oats in Kroger and Remke Markets, they are also sold online through Sam's Clubs and Walmart in twenty-five-pound bags and the normal two-pound bags. This has helped counteract the dip in retail grocery sales.

What's next for pinhead oats? With the prevalence of our regional craft brewers, I'd suggest a Goetta Pinhead Oatmeal Stout, flavored with allspice, nutmeg and perhaps a beef tea. Maybe Rhinegeist, Madtree or Braxton Brewery will take heed.

Chapter 7
GOETTAFEST AND GOETTA CULTURE

*T*here's one thing you won't see at Glier's Goettafest: a salad. But every second weekend in August, in the heat of the summer, you'll see tens of thousands of goetta lovers descending on the Ohio River for four days to eat their beloved local grain sausage. Even in humid, ninety-plus-degree heat, people come to Goettafest to sample the newest concoctions using goetta. People come for the goetta but stay for the fun. It's pure Goetta *Gemutlichkeit*.

Goettafest is one of the big reasons that goetta in greater Cincinnati is still alive over 150 years after its arrival here. Now in its eighteenth year, there is not one, but two Goettafests every summer. Both festivals are the culmination of all things goetta and the generations of families that love and celebrate it.

The mastermind of the event is Mark Balasa, a Cincinnatian of Hungarian descent. Mark tried goetta for the first time on a dare at age sixteen. He became a goetta evangelist and was working for Glier's when he concocted the event in 2001. Mark's purpose was to attract new goetta fans. He claimed that there was a 96 percent conversion rate. Of those who tasted goetta, most came back for more. Now the goetta evangelist works for Queen City Sausage. His idea lives on and has turned into the world's largest goetta event.

The event was born as a small neighborhood festival at Goebel Park in Covington's German Mainstrasse Village. Sponsored by Glier's, original attendee estimates that first year were 2,000. Even with a short rain

Top: A booth at Goettafest 2018 shows the variety of products offered. *Author's collection.*

Right: Poster advertising Glier's Goettafest. *Author's collection.*

shower, the final tally showed 6,000 tri-state goetta lovers attended. True to many German festivals, the original Goettafest crowned a Goetta King and Queen, but the size of the festival has prevented that from continuing. The event outgrew its original location in 2004; now, more than 100,000 people attend the four-day event at Newport's Riverboat Row, with over forty goetta dishes provided by a dozen local restaurants.

The Mainstrasse Village Association until 2018 sponsored the "Original Goettafest," along with Braxon Brewing, in early June at the original location in Goebel Park. The festival extended from Goebel Park along the two-block tree-lined Sixth Street promenade to the Goose Girl Fountain. The festival includes some innovative goetta dishes, like goetta bier cheese slammers, goetta-loaded tater toys, a super pretzel weenie with goetta and goetta corn dogs.

Goetta's cousins in the South and Northeast have their own festivals. The Apple Scrapple Festival happens in early October in Bridgeville, Delaware, and is now in its twenty-seventh year. There are also two Livermush Festivals, one in Shelby, North Carolina, on the third weekend in October, and one in June in Marian, North Carolina, near Asheville. But do they have vending machines or a live mascot walking around for VIP photo ops? No.

Two entertainment stages flank each of the staircases that descend from Newport on the levy in Kentucky to the festival plaza below the flood wall. You'll see the world's only Goetta Vending Machine, where you can get a one-pound tube of every type of goetta Glier's makes—original, hot, bacon and turkey. There's a Goetta Life tent that takes you through the history of goetta, and another that takes you through the history of Glier's. There are children's games involving Mr. Goetta ("The Man of Steel Cut Oats"), the mascot of the Glier's company. In fact, you'll see Mr. Goetta walking around the festival posing for photos. You can take home a plush stuffed version of Mr. Goetta, along with hats, graphic T-shirts, coffee mugs and other Glier's merchandise.

The Glier's Goetta man has been merchandised in items like T-shirts and plush toys. *Author's collection.*

Across from a giant two-story inflated roll of goetta, you can get your picture in

The only goetta vending machine in the world on display at Goettafest 2018. *Author's collection.*

The Yat Ka Mein booth at Goettafest 2018 *Author's collection.*

Goetta mac and cheese has become a Goettafest favorite. *Author's collection.*

front of the Glier's step-and-repeat banner or put your head through a Mr. Goetta character board for a fun photo opp.

You'll see Dan Glier, owner of Glier's, sporting his company baseball cap and blending in like any other goetta lover. But he is in his element and wears a gleeful Cheshire cat grin as he takes in all the people enjoying the product his father, Bob Glier, brought to market in 1946.

A large tent with a picturesque view of the Ohio River and the beautiful Cincinnati skyline is where you can get out of the sun and enjoy your goetta alongside a local craft beer from this year's sponsor, Covington's Braxton Brewery. Why they haven't brewed a Pinhead Oatmeal Goetta Stout for the event is beyond me.

There's the standard goetta fare—goetta, egg and cheese sandwiches, goetta mac and cheese, deep-fried goetta balls and goetta wurst on a bun with sauerkraut. But you'll also see quite a bit of fusion food. Italian-German fusion shows up in goetta pizza, calzones, lasagna and risotto balls. There's Mexican-German fusion, with goetta empanadas, burritos, tacos and tamales. There's the Greek-German fusion, with goetta cheese coneys. Then there's Yat Ka Mein, a Chinese restaurant in Covington that offers the ultimate in German-Chinese fusion. It serves the most dishes, with its goetta fried rice, goetta Rangoon, goetta moo shu taco, spring rolls and goetta lo mein.

If you have a sweet tooth, the goetta sweets are not to be missed. One can try goetta brownies, Goetta Goobers (cake donut holes with bits of goetta) and the ultimate heart-stopper: a grilled goetta burger between two buns of glazed donuts.

GOETTA CULTURE

Aside from the two main goettafests, there are many other opportunities to find goetta in greater Cincinnati. Church festivals, Oktoberfests and other German celebrations like Shutzenfest and Maifest all serve goetta.

Just a few of the Catholic Church festivals that list goetta on their menu are: The Church of the Assumption served goetta dogs and goetta reubens; St. Gertrude Funfest in Madeira served goetta links; and St. Columban of Loveland served goetta burgers. It can also be found in the diets of area religious communities. The Benedictine nuns at St. Walburg were big fans of goetta. When Cincinnati Fransciscan priests Father

Bryant and Father Bruce Hausfield were transferred to Cerillos, New Mexico, to support the Guadalupe Province, they took their mother's goetta recipe with them. Father Bruce made it regularly with Dorsel's pinhead oats shipped in from Cincinnati.

Hamman's Meat Market in Pleasant Run Farms on Old Winton Road has developed quite a few festival customers for its homemade goetta. It supplies the goetta and rye sandwiches at Germania Park's annual Oktoberfest, St. Gabriel Catholic Church's summer festival and the Whitewater Rhinefest at the Harrison, Ohio VFW hall. For the last several years, it's also been supplying goetta for Elder's annual West of the Rhine Plus Wine event in June, where its west parking lot is transformed into a German biergarten with craft brews, German food and bands, like local fave Schnappsband. And you can't have a Catholic festival without gambling. You can have goetta and gamble on games like Beat the Dealer and one of my favorites, the Mug Slide!

Jeffery Finke, of the legacy Finke goetta family, serves his Gourmet Brand Goetta at the June Walton Pigfest in Walton, Kentucky, a fundraiser for St. Joseph Academy.

Outside of the church festivals, goetta has been legitimized at restaurants throughout the city. There are over one hundred restaurants in Cincinnati where you can eat goetta in its purest form as a breakfast meat alongside eggs, pancakes or waffles. All Frisch's locations in Cincinnati serve it as a breakfast item. But then there are other places where you'll see it creatively fused into other dishes.

The first restaurants to embrace goetta were the chili parlors. Many are open late into the night and early morning, so goetta was a natural for them with breakfast. The Cincinnati Dynamic Duo—goetta and eggs—is a popular menu item at the chili parlors. Blue Ash Chili, Chili Time and Pleasant Ridge Chili serve Glier's. Camp Washington Chili serves Queen City Sausage goetta. Price Hill Chili is the only parlor that makes its own goetta in-house. A&A in Mount Healthy and Gourmet Chili in Newport also serve goetta. One Greek establishment, Demetrios Family Restaurant, serves it with egg and cheese in another chili parlor favorite, the double decker.

Frisch's nearly twenty locations in Cincinnati serve goetta at breakfast. One of the most interesting locations to eat goetta is at the Anchor Grill in Covington, nearly directly across the street from the Glier's factory. Patrons can order goetta and eggs twenty-four hours a day while listening to jukebox music and watching homemade automated dioramas of Barbie and Ken dolls. Another interesting place to eat goetta is at Sugar n' Spice in Paddock Hills while you choose a rubber duckie out of a bin as a take-home prize. Other diners serving goetta for breakfast are the Echo and the Hitching Post in Hyde Park, Santorini on the West Side and Tucker's in Over-the-Rhine.

Mike Florea, former chef of Maribelle's, now owns, among other food ventures, Queen City Livestock, which raises Red Wattle and Large Black pigs. The pigs are fed on spent grains from local breweries, rescued restaurant produce and whey from local cheesemakers. Florea served a house recipe of goetta at the restaurant that included head and trotter meat. Queen City Livestock provides the pork for many local restaurants, like Salazar's in Over-the-Rhine, which also serves a housemade goetta with pickled ramps and pistaccio pesto—how elevated!

Goetta pizza is now a thing. The first to introduce it was probably Trotta's Pizza on the West Side on Werk Road. Pizzelli in Mariemont has a wonderful goetta pizza with apple-smoked bacon, fried egg, mozzarella, provolone and maple syrup drizzle. Fessler's Pizza in Newport has a goetta pizza. And the new Catch-a-Fire Pizza in the Madtree Brewery has what it calls its Goettup-Standup Pizza with peppadew peppers, caramelized onion, cracked egg, white cheddar and roasted garlic. Snappy Tomato Pizza has a limited-time goetta and sausage pizza it serves.

Cincinnati's French-born celebrity chef Jean-Robert de Cavel integrates goetta into his daily specials. Goetta Benedict covered with the area's best hollandaise sauce regularly shows up on the menu at his French Crust café in Findlay Market. If goetta is good enough for a former Maisonette five-star chef like Jean-Robert, then it's good enough for anyone, in my opinion.

When the Rookwood Pottery in Mount Adams was open, it had a super-regional dish called Goetta Hanky Panky, a fusion of our cheesy sausge dip and goetta. Blinker's Tavern on Greenup Street in Covington serves a goetta mac and cheese.

Our local fast-food chain, Tom & Chee, which achieved national acclaim by being funded by *Shark Tank*, serves an Armagoetta grilled cheese, with banana, jalapeno and cherry peppers on one slice of rye and another of sourdough.

Some restaurants have gone to naming their goetta dishes after famous locals. Hotel Coppin in Covington has a Roebling Eggs Benedict made with goetta. I wonder if Herr Roebling fueled his suspension bridge–building days with goetta. Big Pappa's café in Milford has the Rosemary Clooney Goetta Omelet. The new Boomtown Biscuits in Pendleton serves a Queen City Bergman, a goetta Scotch egg served with hash and hot cinnamon apples.

A goetta Danish may sound weird to some. But many Cincinnatians dress their goetta with jams and jellies, so the sweet and savory is not so unusual. Skirtz & Johnson Bakery at Findlay Market offered a goetta-apricot Danish that was an absolute delight and sold fast on Saturday and Sunday mornings.

One of the most unique forms of goetta is crafted by Chef Ethan Snider of Fond Lunch and Deli near Harper's Point, who makes his own lamb goetta. He serves it as a sandwich with smoked egg salad and white cheddar on a ciabatta roll. This is not so out-of-the-box, either, considering that in Germany there is a version called *Heidjer Knipp* made of a local special breed of sheep in the Luneburg Heath area near Hanover.

And in July 2019, Moerlein Brewing Company in collaboration with Glier's will introduce the world's first goetta-inspired beer. Moerlein describes it as "a smooth golden lager that features a touch of smoked malt, sea salt, black peppercorn, and pinhead oats provided by Glier's." It will be the official beer of Glier's Goettafest 2019.

There's a whole world of goetta fusion yet to be tried. Could sushi be made from a thin goetta blanket instead of sticky rice? Maybe. What about a goetta Monte Cristo, a goetta shepherd's pie, goetta spaetzle, goetta bahn mi or goetta pad thai? What about goetta ice cream? With our growing Latin American community, maybe a goetta made with chorizo sausage would bring a whole new group into our local goetta-eating population. There is still a wide and blank canvas for more fun goetta creations.

Chapter 8

GOETTA COUSINS IN THE UNITED STATES

THE GERMAN GRUETZWURST DIASPORA

*C*incinnati has the distinction of being the only metropolitan area with German immigrants where a grain sausage proliferated. It's the distinction between a city gruetzwurst and a country gruetzwurst. All other examples of its gruetzwurst cousins come from rural farming areas where German immigrants settled. It's amazing to consider the variety and variation of grain sausages there are in the rural German immigrant regions of the United States. You have to dig, as not every region has a large commercial producer. Some retain their original form from Germany, while others have adapted significantly to their new homes. What this means to goetta is that it has had access to more pork and beef and higher-quality cuts of meats and less organ and other parts used as far back as can be traced in recipes. I have found no family recipes for goetta that include liver, heart or other offcuts of meat.

As a scientist by training, I like to describe natural phenomena in terms of equations. And there is a simple equation for where you will find goetta cousins in the United States. It goes something like this: If an area has a polka band, a dance hall and a local maker of kolache or strudel, it is an area that most likely makes a grain sausage. It can be stated in the form of an equation:

Polka Band + Dance Hall + Kolache/Struedel Makers = Grain Sausage Area

Some examples of this equation are as follows. In Colerain Township, Ohio: the Donauschwaben Hall plus the Alpen Echoes Band plus apple strudel from Servatti's equals goetta, especially at its Oktoberfest. In northwestern Ohio: the Bavarian Haus plus Polka Revolution plus locally made strudel equals an area that makes prettles. In west central Ohio: Minster Oktoberfestplatz plus the Route 161 Wanderers Polka Band plus struedel equals grits. In west central Texas: Weid Hall near Hallettsville plus the Moravians, or the Czechoholics plus pineapple cheese kolache from the Kountry Bakery equals *jitronice*. This can be applied to any area in the United States that has a Germanic immigrant population.

PENNSYLVANIA SCRAPPLE

So I've got a bone to pick with scrapple. Every food writer in the country compares goetta cousins to scrapple. Food writer William Woys Weaver, in his 2003 *Country Scrapple* book, called goetta "oatmeal scrapple!" It's as if scrapple is everywhere and everyone knows what it is. That's a typical coastal mentality. I will give it one point. Scrapple is probably the most American of the Germanic-descended gruetzwursts, because it uses the American grain: cornmeal. But it deserves no more status than its cousins like goetta, livermush, balkenbrij or the many others in the German Gruetzwurst Diaspora. It doesn't even have a great name. It brings up the unsavory subject of the origin of the "scraps" of meat it uses, even though the savvy producers market the ingredients as "pork trimmings" rather than scraps.

Scrapple is also probably the earliest grain sausage in American history. Our Founding Fathers, including President George Washington and Benjamin Franklin, are said to have been fans. It was brought to the Philadelphia, Pennsylvania area before the Revolutionary War, so it has been an American staple for a long time.

Although it originally descended from Anabaptist Germanic immigrants to Pennsylvania from the Palatinate or Lower Rhineland in Germany, it can now be found within a radius that includes the Delmarva Peninsula of Delaware, Maryland, Virginia and Washington, D.C. The Germanic name was *panhaskroppel*, or *panhas*, which was shortened and Anglicanized to scrapple.

A company called Habberstat has been making it commercially since 1863 in Pennsylvania. Rapa started the Delaware scrapple market in the early 1900s, and Hatfield has been making it since 1895 in Pennsylvania. I'm a fan of it. My introduction to it was at Ellen's Coffee Shop in downtown Chestertown, Maryland. Scrapple may have a larger geographic fan base, but I'm loyal to goetta. Scrapple to me has a more minerally taste to it than goetta, with its addition of liver and other organ parts, and a grittier texture, due to the smaller-grained cornmeal. But it does serve as a close second fiddle to goetta at breakfast when visiting the Northeast.

And those in the Northeast have elevated scrapple, like us greater Cincinnatians have done with goetta. They celebrate an Apple Scrapple festival every fall. A minor-league baseball team, the Delmarva Shorebirds, celebrates a Scrapple Day at its field in August. The players sport specialty scrapple jerseys and caps, and scrapple sandwiches are served at the game. Maybe the Reds should consider a Goetta Day at the ballpark.

SOUTHEASTERN INDIANA GRITS

In southeastern Indiana, in the townships around Batesville and Oldenburg, Indiana, goetta is traditionally known as grits. This area, like Cincinnati, has a legacy of German immigrants. These immigrants can be traced back to three areas of the Cradle of Goetta. The town of Huntersville had immigrants from Venne, Engter, Bramsche and surrounding communities north of Osnabruck in the Kingdom of Hanover. The early founders of Oldenburg, Indiana, were from the Catholic parish of Damme, about ten miles farther north of Osnabruck in the Grand Duchy of Oldenburg. This was also where the early families who settled Auglaize County, Ohio's grits country, hailed from. And, many Germanic settlers in Adams and Laughery townships in Indiana came from Heiligenfelde Parish, about forty-five miles northeast in the Kingdom of Hanover, just south of the port city of Bremen.

Oldenburg, Indiana, is a very German town with connections to Cincinnati. It has Village Store, which makes its own homemade goetta, and goetta is served every July at its Freudenfest. Luella Landick Lampert of Oldenburg called the dish "grits" and had been making it since the 1970s when she was interviewed by the *Batesville Herald-Tribune* in 2006. She grew up eating it and learned how to make it from her mother, Josephine Landick. They ate it crisp with potatoes or eggs at breakfast

Several places in Batesville, Indiana, sell grits or goetta. Harmeyer's Meats sells "grits" made from pork and pinhead oats. French's Locker in

Batesville proudly serves goetta. Big Four Café serves goetta as a side, as does Izzy's at the Hillcrest Country Club. Sherman House serves grits at its newly renovated restaurant. And finally, Weiler's Hobo Hut on 1356 State Route 46 in Batesville serves goetta.

In nearby Sunman, Indiana, German grits/goetta are getting harder to find. The two restaurants that used to serve goetta are now closed. The Store Restaurant at the Railroad Crossing served goetta (German grits) and had a Sunday morning buffet. The other, the Old Brick Tavern in Pennsylvania (Penntown), Indiana, on Highway 101, two miles north of Sunman, was known for its goetta sandwiches with hot slaw.

Grits were also common in the early part of the 1900s in the German farming communities around Fort Wayne, Indiana.

MICHIGAN BALKENBRIJ

Over a century ago, thousands of Dutch immigrants settled in cohesive farming communities in western Michigan in Ottowa County, about a third of the way up the peninsula, across Lake Michigan from Milwaukee, Wisconsin. Catholics and Dutch Calvinists had severed ties with the Protestant State Church in 1834 and, by the 1840s, had found life increasingly difficult economically and religiously. The first to settle was Reverend Albertus van Raalte in 1847, near today's Holland, Michigan. And, like a pied piper, he lured other Dutch to the area. Jan Hulst followed in 1847, founding the town of Drenthe. Jan Rabbers soon followed, settling Groningen and New Groningen. Other groups came and settled the surrounding villages of Zeeland, Overisil, Graafschap, Vriesland, Harlem, Noordeloos, New Holland, Staphorst and Zutphen.

These early Dutch immigrants to Michigan spoke in regional dialects and preferred to live among family and friends. Like their Germanic immigrant counterparts in Cincinnati, they fancied themselves citizens of the province they came from—Zeelanders, Groningers, Frisians—not as Dutch. Dutch Catholics, mostly from the province of Brabant, didn't cluster together, so they assimilated into non-Dutch churches, where instruction was in English and Mass was in Latin. It took the next generation to think of themselves as a single ethnic group, except for the Frisians, who continued to isolate themselves from the rest of the Dutch and hold fast to their culture. As the Dutch spread out from the original settlements, they used their unique skills, draining the swamps and farming the rich bottomlands. The Dutch farmhouses, with red and buff-colored brick from the local kilns in Zeeland, can still be seen along the countryside.

They brought with them their favorite foods. One of those dishes was balkenbrij, a cousin of goetta. Unlike goetta, balkenbrij made the trip across the Atlantic with its name and its original recipe intact from the Old World. Balkenbrij is a mix of pork and beef parts, including offal, and bacon, mixed with buckwheat or oatmeal, sometimes blood and sometimes raisins if from the Gelderland. Because of the high level of offal, it was spiced with a special mix, *rommelkruid*, consisting of licorice, sugar, anise, cinnamon, cloves, white pepper, mace, ginger and sandalwood.

It can still be had at the Wooden Shoe Restaurant in Holland, Michigan. The New Holland Brewpub serves it for breakfast with braised red cabbage and eggs sunny-side up. At the Knickerbocker, they serve Hollander Benedict, which is balkenbrij on an English muffin with poached eggs, fried potatoes and beer hollandaise. At the Farmhouse restaurant in Zeeland, Michigan, it is served as a side with toast. For those wanting to serve it at home, it can be found in the refrigerated section of Wierson's Central Park Foods in Holland, Michigan. It can also be found alongside a lineup of Dutch pastries at DeBoer's Bakery in Zeeland.

LIVERMUSH

Livermush is the goetta cousin that the people of western North Carolina go hog wild for. Draw a line through Mecklenburg County northwest to Guilford and Rockingham Counties. If you grew up west of that line, you know livermush. It was brought to the southern Appalacian Piedmont region by frontiersmen and -women who emigrated from Germany by way of Pennsylvania. That explains its similarity to scrapple. They would have brought with them a taste for liverwurst, a pork meat and liver smoked sausage that traditionally contained bacon. It isn't hard to imagine liverwurst evolving into livermush in a frontier setting, since it is both easier to prepare—the meat is boiled, so there's no smoker to maintain—and requires less meat, using cornmeal and flour as a filler.

It's made of at least 30 percent pork liver, head parts and cornmeal, spiced heavily with pepper and sage. Like goetta, it's sliced and panfried, served alongside grits and eggs at breakfast. It's also typically served as a quick

Livermush made in North Carolina. *Author's collection.*

lunch-on-the-go sandwich with mayonnaise or mustard and nestled into a southern biscuit. It's an institution in North Carolina, with several Livermush Festivals, the largest one in Shelby, forty-five minutes west of Charlotte, and smaller ones in Drexel and Marion. And, like goetta, it has found its way into other dishes outside of breakfast, like pizza.

Part of the recent popularity of livermush is due to commercial producers like Mack's and Jenkins Foods, a mile away from each other, who between them make forty-five thousand pounds of it a week. B.P. (short for Benjamin Plato) Jenkins ran a general store with his brother outside Shelby. When the Depression closed the store in the early 1930s, he began thinking about what he could sell to the stores that remained.

Jenkins and his wife had always kept livestock—dairy cows, chickens and hogs—to feed their family. "The couple was pretty self-sufficient," Harry Mauney, current owner of Jenkins' Foods, says. Using his family's recipe, Jenkins started cooking up livermush in bulk in a big cast-iron pot over a wood fire. At first, he sold it out of the trunk of his car. In 1933, thanks to livermush's familiarity and its very low cost—about eight times less than bacon—B.P. Jenkins stumbled into a market with a lot of pent-up demand. He wasn't alone in spotting the opportunity. Many others got into the business. At one point, there were four families within an eight-mile radius making a living selling livermush,

Earl Scruggs, the father of bluegrass music, who recorded the first bluegrass song, "Foggy Mountain Breakdown," at Cincinnati's Herzog Studios in 1949, is a big fan of livermush.

South Carolina has a version that's thickened with rice and sometimes called liver pudding, or scrabblin' mush.

BOUDIN

Yes, even Cajun boudin is a cousin of goetta. It's estimated that 80 percent of the boudin purchased in Louisiana is consumed before the buyer leaves the parking lot. Most of the rest is polished off in the car. So, Cajun boudin rarely gets out of the state, or even the home, for that matter. Unlike goetta, it's a food of convenience, already packaged in a natural casing and meant to be eaten on the go. Boudin and a Coke is the Cajun breakfast of champions in Louisiana.

Boudin is a grain sausage made of rice, pork trimmings—including heart and liver—onions, green peppers and seasonings, all ground and stuffed into a natural casing. It's steamed or heated for on-the-spot gnoshing. Regional variations exist from parish to parish and from neighborhood to neighborhood, but the best versions come from the specialty meat shops, grocery stores and restaurants that make it in-house. Some of the best of these makers are to be found in gas stations or convenience stores with their own kitchen.

It is to be found in the region known as Acadiana or Cajun Country, in an area centered in Lafayette, Louisiana, and extending out in a twenty-five-mile radius—about a two-hour drive west of New Orleans. As Cincinnatians are with goetta, Cajuns are obsessive about their boudin, having long discussions about the crispness of the casing, the rice-to-meat ratio, eating method, spice levels, best texture and just how much liver to include. Boudin inspires fond memories of good times with family and friends and discussions about whose recipe is the best.

Like goetta, it's nearly impossible to discover the precise historical origin of Louisiana's boudin. But we do know that it traces its porcine lineage, like the Cajun people, back to France. The French eat a sausage called *boudin blanc* ("white sausage"), similar in name only. The French version is

Left: Boudin balls are a delicacy in Louisiana. *Author's collection.*

Right: Lafayette, Louisiana, hosts a boudin cookoff every year. *Author's collection.*

highly perishable, made with pork, chicken and/or veal and mixed with milk, cognac and spices. When the French Acadians (today's Cajuns) hightailed it out of Nova Scotia, Canada, after being thrown out by the Brits in 1755, they adapted their foodways and traditions to their new surroundings in the bayous, prairies and backwoods of Louisiana. This required grit, flexibility and, of course, creativity. So, at slaughter time, when they aimed to use every part of the animal, it wasn't a stretch for the Cajuns to call this what they had always called sausage: boudin. Mix in the sausage-making talents of the German immigrants who flooded southwest Louisiana in the 1720s and the large-scale rice production at the end of the nineteenth century, and you end up with Cajun boudin. Today, in places like St. Martinville, at La Grand Boucherie des Cajuns—the communal hog butchering—held the Sunday before Mardi Gras, or the Coup de Gras, as Cajuns call it, the old practice of making boudin is embraced, and the custom and community spirit continue to be passed to the next generation.

There is even a Boudin Trail Brochure, sponsored by the Lafayette Chamber of Commerce, which lists and describes nearly fifty producers of boudin. There are only a few who still make boudin rouge, the blood version, like the Babineaux brothers of Breaux Bridge. Modern health codes have made this process too complex to be profitable for most producers who don't have their own slaughterhouse. And while most add pork liver, Tiny (Damon) Prudhomme, nephew of famous and award-winning chef Paul Prudhomme, former owner of K-Paul's Restaurant in New Orleans, omits liver, saying it imparts too strong and polarizing a flavor. At his House of Meat in Broussard, Louisiana, he keeps his customers happy with his unique nonlivery-flavored boudin.

Like goetta, boudin is an immigrant sausage that has its origins at the time of slaughter to use up all cuts of the pig. It's a pork-only slaughter sausage that uses rice instead of pinhead oats as the grain extender. It's descended from the French sausages boudin blanc (contains no pig blood) and boudin rouge (which does), but it's very different from the boudin you'll find in Europe.

Each October, there is a Boudin Cookoff in Lafayette, where all makers congregate to show off and compete with their home-grown recipes. And there is even a secret, all-male society, called Boudin for Peace, that goes on a boudin-tasting excursion every year on the Saturday before Mardi Gras.

Boudin balls are popular bite-sized versions of the sausage. I tasted some housemade boudin balls this October at B&C Cajun Restaurant in Vacherie, St. James Parish, Louisiana. They have a similar texture and taste to goetta but definitely have a strong liver flavor. New forms of boudin, including seafood, alligator and smoked versions, continue to pop up.

Upper Midwestern Gritzwurst

In the Upper Midwest, in Germanic immigrant farming regions of Wisconsin, Minnesota, North Dakota, Michigan, east-central Illinois and even Perry County, Missouri, gritswurst was traditionally made on the farm from the meat of a boiled hog's head. The meat was ground, spiced with cinnamon and allspice or pepper and sage and then mixed with steel cut oats. Some variations added dark raisins, a version that has ancestors in northern Germany. Others used pearl barley as the grain, because that was available, or in addition to steel-cut oats. In the Dakotas, the Hutterite religious communities have a recipe that uses hog's head and buckwheat grouts. It is called gritzwurst, gritza and even gritzelwurst across the Upper Midwest.

Places that have gritzwurst in Minnesota are within a fifty-mile radius in a semicircle from Minneapolis. Some of those places are Machenthun's Meat Market in St. Bonifacious, Huettl's Butcher Shop in Lake City, Bev's Café in Red Wing, Randell's Smokehouse in New Ulm and Lang's Meats in Glencoe.

Other places in the Midwest that serve gritswurst are in St. Joseph, Michigan, just south of Dutch balkenbrij country; the West End Tavern & Grocery in Frohna, Missouri; and in Kenosha, Wisconsin.

OSTFRIESAN BLUTGRITZWURST

In east central Illinois, the communities that were settled by Ostfriesans, from the province of Germany just north of Oldenburg, have traditions of blood grain sausages made at the time of slaughter that utilize the pork head, blood and a grain extender. Three Ostfriesean recipes for this goetta cousin are included in the *Recipes from Oma and Opa's Kitchen*, compiled by the Ostfriesan Heritage Society of East Central Illinois. One uses hog head, liver, heart and tongue with flour; another uses oatmeal, graham flour, head meat and "grebens," or skin with lard; and another uses grebens, rye or wheat flour and white bread. All recipes call for the addition of milk as an extender, which no other grain sausages—with or without blood—call for. This emparts a creamier texture to the sausage. All recipes call for the blood sausage to be sliced, fried and drizzled in syrup.

Another recipe in the Ostfriesian cookbook, called koppkees or head cheese, is more similar to our goetta and not like the jelled head cheese we know of as Schwartenmagen. This recipe calls for hog head meat, liver, heart, tongue and pearl barley.

Virlon Suits recalled in the cookbook what butchering day was like for German farm families in Illinois in the 1940s and '50s and how little of the animal was wasted:

> *Butchering day was one of the highlights of my young life in the forties and fifties. The term butchering day is a broad term and actually covers a two-day event, particularly in the case of beef and pork. After the animal was killed, it was "stuck" almost immediately to drain off the blood. In the case of the porker the blood was caught or captured with a bread pan and was used to make blood sausage. The steer's head and entrails were disposed of, but the hog head was saved for head cheese.*

Some of the pork fat would be diced for use in making the blood sausage. The hog head would be cooked and all the meat trimmed off, ground up and made into head cheese. Several recipes exist for making this. Some people incorporated ground-up liver. However, my parents generally did not use the liver but instead mixed the hog head meat with barley grain to give it substance and body.

TEXAS JITRNICE AND IOWA JATERNICE

In east central Texas, about halfway between San Antonio and Houston, is the center of jitrnice country. The sausage of the former Austro-Hungarian Empire is kin to our goetta. Jitrnice (pronounced "yee-ter-neet-za") is known within about a twenty-five-mile radius around the town of Schulenburg, at the intersection of I-77 and I-10. This is the area where Czech-speaking and German-speaking immigrants from the former Austro-Hungarian Empire—the provinces of Moravia and Bohemia—settled from the 1840s to the 1870s to find a better life, many to escape poverty, famine and army conscription. They were referred to as "bohunks" by the native Texans, a derogatory term mixing Bohemian and Hungarian and meaning "hillbilly." They first built churches, typically Catholic, and then dance halls or Turner or Sokol Halls for gymnastics and athletics. The area is spotted with historic dance halls, beautiful folk-painted Catholic churches and a few nine-pin bowling alleys, called "kegel." A wonderful tour called the Painted Churches of Schulenburg is a great day trip from Austin or San Antonio. Between the end of August and November, there are more than thirty German/Czech festivals in the area.

We've all heard of Tex-Mex cuisine. But in this area of Texas, there's another brand of cuisine that's best named Tex-Czech. It's the foodway of these Germanic and Slavic immigrants from the former Austro-Hungarian Empire in the current Czech Republic. Mix some of these cuisines with local chili powder, and it becomes Czech-Mex. There has been a *Czhilispeil*, or chili cookoff, forty-six years running in Flatonia, Texas, denoting a definite Czech-style chili that might include a spicy Czech sausage or even jitrnice. So jitrnice sausage is deeply embedded in this German-Czech foodway but is becoming less known as generations separate from the original Czech-speaking immigrants. One of the most visible food items in the Tex-Czech foodway is the fruit-filled kolache, a less-buttery and dense

An image of Maeker's jitrnice in sausage form, made in Shiner, Texas. *Courtesy of Maeker's.*

love child of the croissant and Danish roll. The kolache travels well outside of Texas and has even recently made an infiltration into the Cincinnati market through United Dairy Farmers and small coffee shops like Mad Llama in Madisonville, Ohio. There is also a savory version of the kolache that is typically stuffed with a spicy sausage or another savory filling like shredded chicken or barbecue. It's called the *koblasnick*. To my knowledge, there is no jitrnice-filled koblasnik.

People who grew up eating jitrnice are passionately addicted to it, just like those of us in the Cult of Goetta. Jitrnice, like goetta, was originally a slaughter sausage, designed as the catch-all recipe that ensures use of "everything but the squeal." The Czechs of Texas call this celebration at hog slaughter *zabijacka*. It's very similar to Cajun boudin sausage from Louisiana, made with rice, which is sometimes included with barley in jitrnice. In Cajun Country, the hog slaughter celebration is called the *boucherie*.

In Czech, the word *jitra* means "liver," so it's probably a reference to the sausage's liver content. Another Czech dialect calls the sausage *jaternice*. But another observation is that the Czech word *jatra* means "morning," and typically, the sausage is eaten as a breakfast food, so maybe it is the derivation of the form jaternice or *jatranice*.

Jitrnice eaters stay true to their recipes, some vehemently leaving out ingredients found in other versions, never going outside their ancestral box. Jitrnice is a sausage originally made from pork head and tongue, snouts, pork offal (heart, lungs, liver, kidneys) and beef hearts and kidney, along with rice and barley. A lot of the butchers compare it to Cajun boudin, the way some compare goetta to scrapple. Older recipes call for boiling the pig's head to remove the meat, but newer recipes use pork shoulder and better cuts of pork. It's typically spiced with paprika, marjoram and heavy garlic. Meat is cooked and ground, and it is either linked in a sausage or poured into pans in porridge form and then panfried crispy like goetta, then served with baked potatoes and beets. Texans like to say "fry it like hash," whereas in Cincy we know exactly how to panfry goetta—thin and crispy. There is no need to specify.

I had the great opportunity to travel from the town of West to Hallettsville, and then east to Shiner, interviewing about ten Czech butchers along the way. Although West has three large kolache bakeries whose meat counters serve Czech sausages—Slovacek, Little Czech Bakery and Gerik's—none carried jitrnice. The young butcher at Slovacek's knew what jitrnice was and said they made it at home but not for the store.

I learned from Brian Prause at the 122-year-old Prause's Meats in La Grange, Texas, that butchers are no longer allowed by the USDA to use pork lung in their jitronice, because of health concerns. Many now call it head sausage, as few recognize the Czech name. The Prause family used to make jitronice, but since it's an all-day process, they no longer can spare the time. They do make some spectacular smoked and nonsmoked Czech sausages. Smithfield Meat Locker to the west of La Grange used to make jitrnice but no longer does. The Texas Czech Heritage and Cultural Center in La Grange has a large collection of Czech cookbooks with generations-old jitrnice recipes from the area.

Paddy Magliolo at Willie Joe's Processing in High Hill, Texas, who makes the beloved High Hill Sausage for St. Mary's Annual Labor Day German Picnic, says they spice their own jitrnice with salt, pepper and garlic, use rice only, as well as pork trim and "some pork organs," which he wouldn't specify.

The City Market in Schulenburg, owned by the Czech Smrkovsky family, makes jitrnice in the cold weather months starting in October, but they do not add liver, as it's very strong, and not everyone is a fan. The largest concentration of meat markets that make jitrnice that I encountered on my Jitrnice Road Tour is along I-90 between Halletsville and Shiner. Janak's makes it year-round in block form, unlinked, but calls it head sausage.

Maeker's, in Shiner, which has been in business since 1967, makes it year-round in their processing plant near the Spoetzl Brewery. Founders Tinky and Martha Maeker sold the business in 2015 to Douglas and Melanie Pevlud, who use Douglas's grandfather's one-hundred-year-old Czech recipe for jitrnice. I can't imagine a better accompaniment to jitrnice than a Shiner

Bock made at Spoetzl. Patek's Market in Shiner next to Saints Cyril and Methodius Church also makes it year-round in both linked and block form, but they call it head sausage.

This slaughter sausage is not just a product of the Texas Czech communities. It's also to be found in Iowa, Minnesota and even Wisconsin's Czech communities. Like the Texas Czech immigrants, many of these immigrants came to the United States from the 1840s to the 1870s from the Kingdom of Moravia, very near the border of today's Slovakia, an area known as Wallachia. There's a town in east central Texas country by that name. The people are said to be Moravian Vlachs, speaking a distinct Czech dialect with a Slovak accent. Also part of this immigration were ethnic Germans whose ancestors settled the forested regions of Bohemia, Moravia and the former Austro-Hungarian Empire.

Recipes for jaternice from Iowa and the Midwest call for salt, pepper and marjoram and typically use barley as the grain, rather than rice, which is commonly used in Texas. Texas recipes call for just salt and pepper and maybe garlic but usually include sauteed onions. In Texas, the meat is also a coarser grind with more seasoning than it is in the midwestern states. Many describe the flavor as tasting overwhelmingly of liver. Some prefer the cartilaginous aspect of the pork head meat. Some versions, like that made in Minnesota, use a high amount of liver, offering a darker-looking version more akin to what we call liver pudding in Cincinnati.

Although it's getting harder to find, as legacy butchers go out of business, there are still some places it can be found in the Midwest. Polashek's Locker Service in Provatin, Iowa, uses barley for theirs and says it contains ears, snouts, cheeks and tongues. In an episode of *Bizarre Eats*, Andrew Zimmern made them famous with a visit. Nolachecks, in Thorp, Wisconsin, also uses barley, snouts and skin, and theirs is darker than the Texas and Iowa varieties. New Prague, Minnesota, has a few meat markets carrying it. Perkarna's Meat Market in Jordan, Minnesota, calls it jiternice. In Minnesota, it's eaten for breakfast with cottage cheese, hasbrowns, scrambled eggs or kolaches. Many also serve it with toasted *houska*, the Czech *brötchen* (braided bread, crusted with poppy, caraway or sea salt).

Whether it's with rice or barley, or more offal or more liver, jaternice is another sibling in our Goetta family tree.

JOHNNY-IN-THE BAG AND BEUTELWURST

We must also mention Johnny-in-the-Bag, or, as it's known in Germany, beutelwurst. In addition to containing blood, it is different from goetta in that it uses rye as the grain instead of pinhead oats, giving it a more gritty texture than goetta. It has quite a different taste than goetta, more minerally and more fatty tasting.

This sausage has to be made very close to slaughter time, as the blood congeals fast, or an anti-coagulant has to be added to the blood. It's typically pressed into a linen bag, thus the name. The diameter is larger than a typical sausage, more the diameter of a luncheon meat roll.

Commercial producers like H.H. Meyers provided Johnny-in-the-Bag to Greater Cincinnatians. And nearly every meat stall in Findlay Market carred it. In 1936, a local chain, Pay 'N Takit, advertised the blood sausage as "a savory breakfast." Like goetta, Johnny-in-the-Bag is sliced and panfried. Grocery retailer Kroger advertised it as early as 1907 in its lineup of sausage products.

Although it's clear that Johnny-in-the-Bag is a descendant of beutelwurst, it's not known where the name came from. There is a Dutch nonmeat pudding called Jan-in-die-sac. But the name doesn't seem to exist outside of the greater Cincinnati area. It seems this term was invented by a Cincinnati Germanic butcher before the turn of the twentieth century.

The blood sausage is slowly dying off as meat markets stray away from using blood because of restrictive regulations. Stehlin's is the only meat market in Cincinnati that makes Johnny-in-the-Bag commercially, and they usually make it seasonally, in the colder months.

Chapter 9

THE OHIO GOETTA-GRITS-PRETTLES TRAIL

Many have heard of the Bourbon Trial in Kentucky, or the Ohio Ice Cream Trail, or even the Butler County Donut Trail. But we have a trail in Ohio of related German gruetzwursts. It follows the path of the former Miami and Erie Canal, which roughly follows Interstate 75 today. The 248-mile canal was completed in 1845, and its path went from Cincinnati, through Dayton, Piqua, Minster, New Bremen, St. Mary's, Delphos and Defiance to Toledo.

This obscure trail has stops in three counties that had historic Germanic immigrant settlements. The stops on the trail are Hamilton, Auglaize and Henry Counties. Goetta is native to Hamilton County, grits are native to Auglaize County and prettles are native to Henry County. But they all hail from the same general area in northwestern Germany, the Cradle of Goetta, and are very similar in ingredients, namely, that they are all made from pinhead oats and contain pork and/or beef.

The great thing about Auglaize and Henry Counties is that their German immigrants came from very specific areas of Germany and were propagated by chain migration from those areas. As a result, we can trace the origin of grits and prettles to the common grain sausage of those areas more easily than we can trace goetta back to a specific regional grain sausage. The Germanic immigrants to Auglaize County came in the 1830s and 1840s and were part of two groups: Catholics from near Oldenburg, and Lutherans from Hanover and Westphalia. The immigrants to Henry County and the area around Napoleon, Ohio,

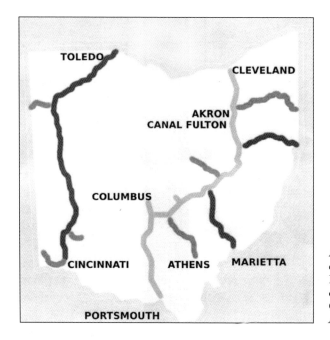

A map showing the route of the former Miami and Erie Canal and the route of the Ohio Goetta-Grits-Prettles Trail. *Author's collection.*

came from a very specific region around the village of Visselhovede in the former Kingdom of Hanover.

Cincinnati was a large metropolitan city and as such had much more diversity in its German immigrants. They came from nearly all the former kingdoms of Germany. Cincinnati German immigrants came not only from northern Germany but also from other kingdoms, like Alsace-Lorraine, Bavaria, the Rhineland, the Palatinate and even Switzerland, so it is much harder to trace the specific regional origin of goetta. One thing is sure: if we could find the regional Plattdeutsch dialect that goetta was a part of, we could pinpoint its location. The largest clue for us is the name. But that is also the hardest part, because the dialect from which *goetta* came could possibly be dead now.

MINSTER OHIO GRITS

Auglaize County is in west-central Ohio, near the Indiana state border. It's shaped like a handgun pointing east and is about an hour or so north of Dayton, Ohio. The southwest corner, where the German immigrant concentration exists, is the handle of the gun.

The highest point on the Miami and Erie Canal was in Auglaize County. In 1845, German and Irish immigrants completed the construction of the twenty-three-mile canal stretch in Minster–New Bremen–Lockington (now Piqua). This brought a minimum of two hundred canalboats through the canal every hour, day and night. Four Germanic immigrant communities are situated on this summit: Fort Loramie, Minster, New Bremen and New Knoxville. This is the heart of German grits eaters. All of these towns in one way or another had connection with the Miami and Erie Canal.

Immigrants to Minster and Fort Laramie were Catholics from southern Oldenburg around the parish of Damme, in the towns of Langforden (about eighteen miles north of Damme), Holdorf (two miles west of Damme), Bakum (fifteen miles north of Damme) and Twistringen (twenty miles northeast of Damme). This area was surrounded by moors or swamps.

Those who came to New Bremen were Protestants from Hanover, and those who settled New Knoxville were Protestants from the Westphalian village of Ladbergen, halfway between Munster and Osnabrook in a region called Tecklenburg, or the Westphalian Graftshaft. New Knoxville has been studied by linguists because it had its own Plattdeutsch dialect that is different from that of Minster and New Bremen, collectively called the Ohio Platt. When Ohio State University language department professor Wolfgang Fleischauer played recordings of Auglaize County Plattedeutsch to Germans from the regions where the original settlers came, they said, "Our grandfathers talked like that. No one talks like that anymore." This is another indication that the old Plattdeutsch dialect from which *goetta* came has died out as well.

Minster, Ohio, has strong ties to the Cincinnati northern German immigrant population. The town was founded in 1832 by the utopian socialist Franz Joseph Stallo, who was living in Cincinnati at the time with his four children. Herr Stallo was an immigrant from the Damme, near Oldenburg and near where the Finkes came from in Neunkirken-Voerden. While living in Westphalia, Stallo had drained the Voerden Moor, burned the turf and planted buckwheat, a practice that would spread throughout northern German farming communities. Thus, the area's gruetzwurst would have commonly included buckwheat as the grain adder. Stallo, along with six other agents, were representing a group of about ninety Catholic German immigrants who came via Cincinnati. As a schoolteacher, bookbinder and printer, Stallo distributed a poem praising the newfound freedoms of America to folks back home in Hanover and Oldenburg. We may have Stallo to thank for bringing the families who brought goetta to

An image of the Miami and Erie Canal in Minster, Ohio. *Courtesy of Public Library of Cincinnati and Hamilton County.*

Ohio. By 1843, the Miami and Erie Canal had connected Minster to the Ohio River—and to the *Goettakreis*, or region of goetta-eating Cincinnatians and northern Kentuckians.

Early suggestions for names of the new German settlement—New Twistringen, New Osnabruck and New Damme—suggested the villages in Goetta-Grits Country where the families had immigrated. They chose Stallotown, to honor its founder, but then after his death, it was changed to Muenster, or Minster, another town represented by the founding families.

The connection to Cincinnati continued after Stallotown's founding. The archbishop of Cincinnati, Reverend John Baptist Purcell, sent the first priest, Father Johann Wilhelm Horstmann, an immigrant from Glandorf,

Osnabruck, Germany, in 1833 to minister to the early Catholic pioneer families of Stallotown/Minster and the nearby immigrant community of New Glandorf. Minster's German Catholic community formed the parish of St. Augustine, and New Glandorf's formed St. John the Baptist's parish with Father Horstmann's leadership. In 2014, the Archdiocese of Cincinnati, Ohio's Catholic Rural Life of St. Mary's and Sidney Deaneries created a Catholic Century Farms Registry and awarded the designation to twenty-four family farms in the Minster area that had been continually farming for the last one hundred years. One family, Urban and Mary Louise Enneking Seger, trace their farm back to an original Goetta-Grits Country pioneer, Johann Enneking, who founded the farm between 1833 and 1835.

There's even a Covington-Minster connection. The beloved Covington artist Frank Duveneck's mother, Katherine Siemers Duveneck, was part of the early settlers of Stallotown/Minster. After both of her parents died in the same cholera epidemic as Stallo, she and her sister, now orphans, walked all the way from Minster to Covington, Kentucky, where some of their family friends had stayed. Katherine Duveneck's granddaughter-in-law, Josephine Duveneck, even documented in her book *Frank Duveneck: Painter-Teacher*, a primitive form of gruetzwurst or grits that the Siemers family liked. They made a sort of loaf of fat mixed with cornmeal that was steamed in cheesecloth. The Duveneck family, being of good German working-class stock, probably embraced the goetta that was made in the area and would fuel the young creative Duveneck as he painted neighborhood signs and church interiors.

James Knox Lytle platted the village of Knoxville in 1836. One couple, Wilhelm and Elisabeth Fledderjohann Kuckhermann, immigranted from Ladbergen in northwest Germany, near the border of the Netherlands. They missed their boat to St. Louis, so they settled in Minster and New Bremen, ending up in New Knoxville. The couple wrote home to their families, and from 1835 to 1850, a group of Ladbergen families—the Fledderjohanns, Meckstroths and Lutterbecks—came in a chain migration. Ladbergen sat on the Dortmund-Ems Canal, so immigrants were experienced with canal construction and helped with construction and upkeep of the Miami and Erie Canal.

New Bremen, Ohio, was founded mostly by Hanoverians, who, like Minster's founders, came to the United States via Cincinnati. On July 23, 1832, a group of thirty-three Hanoverian immigrants who arrived in Cincinnati formed a group called the City of Bremen Society. Together, they drew up a charter to authorize purchasing land to found a Protestant town somewhere in Ohio. The group found eighty acres of land at the highest point of the brand-new Miami and Erie Canal, which was nearing completion. In honor of their homeland, they named this new community Bremen.

Today, the largely Catholic village of Minster, on Interstate 75, celebrates its German immigrant heritage with one of the largest—and probably the most authentic—German Oktoberfests in Ohio, during the first weekend in October. Authentic German foods, polka dancing and beer-carrying competitions are some of the highlights of Minster's celebration.

A few years ago, I had the opportunity to taste grits in Minster. I was on the way to meet some friends for a weekend at Indian Lake, only three exits north of Minster, Ohio. So, what better test situation for grits than a Cincinnati contingent familiar with goetta.

I took exit 99 off of Interstate 75, drove through the little town of Anna, then twelve more miles into the very German American Minster, Ohio. I drove through downtown and headed toward the towering twin spires of St. Augustine Catholic Church. I thought this would be the epicenter of grits-eating Minsterites and a good place to start to ask about a local meat market I might find these grits.

Nearly adjacent to the large, beautiful, red-brick church is Oktoberfestplatz, straddling Minster's main street. A large expanse of lawn with a beautiful bandstand gazebo will be the site of a massive celebration of German American food and culture in October. I am told that many people will party on Saturday afternoon, go to Mass at St. Augustine to slow down their buzz and then party on into the night after church lets out. I think that sounds like the best way to go to church in the fall—straddle it with an Oktoberfest!

I was lucky to find a Wagner's IGA just one block up from Oktoberfestplatz. I thought that, surely, if they didn't have grits, they'd at least know where I might find some. I walked in and went immediately to the deli counter and asked a girl of about seventeen where I might find the local German grits or meat grits. She looked confused and asked some of the other teenage workers if they had German or meat grits. When they all looked like I had two heads with horns, I asked if there was a nearby local meat market. They said "no." If it wasn't for a smart teenage guy who heard my conversation, I would never have found the grits. He said, "Are you just looking for grits?" I told him I was, and he led me to a corner of the meat section where there was a mother lode.

They sold them in one-and-a-half and half-pound increments, shrink-wrapped. The sticker read, "Wagner's Signature Recipe—Our Own

Grits—(Pork , Beef, Salt, Pepper, and Pin Oats)." So I knew these would be authentic. I decided to go big and bought the one-and-a-half-pound package for nearly five dollars. Pork and beef prices have skyrocketed this year, but this was for a fun lake weekend, and a special treat, so no worries.

I showed the girl at the meat counter who had looked at me funny when I asked her for meat grits the package I had chosen. She said, "Oh yeah, we just call them grits." I paid for my proud find and asked for a bag of ice. The counter girl paged another kid, who looked like he was ten (but I'm sure was about seventeen, like the rest of the crew) to help me with an ice bag outside. As he unlocked the ice chest, I told him I'd found the infamous Minster grits that in southern Ohio we called goetta and was excited to try them with other southern Ohio goetta experts at Indian Lake. He looked at me quietly with a look that said, "Whatever, old dude."

Armed with my find, I drove off to Indian Lake to enjoy pizza, beer and a beautiful sunset over the lake. The next morning, after everyone was up and had their coffee, we made a big breakfast with eggs, French toast and Minster grits. The taste testers were all familiar with goetta, its nuances, prep methods and how to dress it best.

I cooked the grits in small rectangular pieces in an iron skillet over low heat. What I found was that the pieces kind of fell apart in the pan, and this made them hard to brown. I did get some brown on the sides, but not as much as we typically get with goetta. The flavor was ok, although not as oniony and spicy as the homemade goetta I'm used to. I ate them without any condiment dressing, to taste the flavor. The whole mix seemed mushier and blander, overall, but a good substitute for homemade goetta in a pinch.

There is one main difference between Cincinnati Goetta and Minster grits. Linda Enneking summed it up: "I don't think you will ever be able to persuade people around Minster to add onion to their grits. The only seasonings are salt and pepper, as shown on the label. If you are careful when you cook grits and don't stir very much, you can get them to brown nicely. A piece of toast with grape jelly goes well with grits, or pancakes and syrup." Minster grits also do not employ allspice, like we do in our goetta in Cincinnati, perhaps because of scarity or expense in rural Ohio. Because of the lack of onions, Minster grits will probably taste bland to most Cincinnati goetta lovers.

A Mrs. Amelia Freytag, born in 1887, of Fort Laramie, Ohio, told the *Cincinnati Enquirer* in 1968 that grits were prepared in the old country to use up pork head meat. Freytag's German immigrant grandparents settled three miles from Minster, Ohio. Some people then called them hafer grits, which

Grits are made at Wagner's IGA in Minster, Ohio. *Author's collection.*

translates to "oat grits." Freytag said that grits were a common meal in the early German settlements at Celina, New Bremen and Minster.

Stephanie Heitkamp makes the grits for Wagner's IGA. She says they've been making Wagner's Signature Storemade Grits for over eighty years with the German-American family recipe of the founder, A.J. Wagner. A.J. Wagner opened the first Wagner's grocery in 1922 at 91 West Fourth Street. The original grocery served as a general store, even selling religious items like Sacred Heart and Mary statues for front yards. Wagner's IGA is now a third-generation-owned business, with grandson Wally Wagner Jr. taking the helm. Their customers range in age, but most are local to the stores, or have friend or family ties to the area. In addition to the Wagner's IGA in Minster, there are Wagner's locations in Fort Laramie (established 2003) and in New Bremen (2013), in Auglaize County.

Many in the area of Minster claim the best Minster grits were made by Woehrmyer's Meat Market, which closed in the mid-1990s and was owned by Bill Woehrmyer. The recipe Bill used, that of his mother Vera Puthoff Woehrmeyer, is preserved in the 2010 Minster Historical Society's *Heart and Heritage Cookbook.*

Woehrmeyer Grits (Vera Puthoff Woehrmyer)

2.5 pounds pork shoulder
2.5 pounds beef chuck roast
1 pound fresh side meat
1.5 pounds pinhead oats
Salt and pepper

Season the meat and boil in a covered kettle until done, until it falls off the bone. Remove from kettle, but save the broth. In the liquid left from the meat, cook the pin oats about 45 minutes, stirring often so it will not stick. Grind the meat and add the pin oats. Cook about half an hour. Add more water if necessary. Pour mixture into loaf pans and let cool. Slice and fry.

Another legacy producer of German grits was Ripploh Meats in Minster, Ohio, founded by William Ripploh in 1887 and passed to his son Joseph Ripploh, and then to his grandon William. The elder William Ripploh's parents were part of the first Germanic immigrant families of Minster, arriving via Cincinnati in 1855. Ripploh Meats advertised fresh grits in a 1943 *Minster Post* newspaper. They got their steers from local farmers like Henry Schmiesing, Frank Niemeyer and Frank Boyer, had them slaughtered at the Minster Meat Locker and provided the products to local homes and restaurants, like the Wooden Shoe Inn. A.W. Boecker Meat and Grocery also made grits in the 1940s.

Winner's Meats in Osgood, Ohio, also makes its own grits. It was founded in 1928 by Robert Winner. The third generation of the Winner family, led by president Brian Winner, is carrying on the tradition. The product page for grits on its website reads: "The homemade pork meat grits you remember! Our German cousins in Cincinnati call this goetta!" It shows a very appetizing, crispy-fried, rectangular slice of grits lying on top of scrambled eggs, with two slices of bacon. Winner's supplies its meats to about thirty-four stores from Route 33 south to Dayton, Ohio, including the German Bremenfest in mid-August in the town of New Bremen.

Morrie's Landing is a Caribbean-themed restaurant in Fort Laramie State Park on the lake, with a dock and outdoor patio. It serves Minster grits in its restaurant to hungry lake-goers and campers.

Kah Meats, a fifth-generation-owned meat market in Wapokoneta at 728 Keller Drive, makes its own grits. They've been butchering hogs and beef since 1898, so they definitely have all the parts to use for grits.

There doesn't seem to be a common way to dress Minster's meat grits, as is done with Cincinnati goetta with ketchup, grape jelly or maple syrup. But there is one additon to a breakfast of Minster's meat grits that one would find: a delicious piece of zweiback, perhaps compliments of Kuehne's Bakery. Zweiback is a hard, north German pastry, like the Italian biscotti, meant for dunking in your coffee. This may indicate an origin from around Bremen, where knipp is served with zweiback.

Grits eaters spill out into Mercer and Shelby Counties in Ohio, as well. In Findlay, Ohio, in Hancock County, which is almost halfway between Auglaize County grits population and the Henry County prettles population, people call it hafer grits. *Hafer* is the German word for "oats." They're also called hava and hobble grits, which are both misheard interpretations of *hafer* from second and third generations hearing the term from older relatives. One restaurant in Findlay, the Dark Horse, has hafer grits on its breakfast menu.

About ten miles due west of Fort Laramie, Ohio, is the small town of Burkettsville, Ohio, in Mercer Couunty, where the only canned goetta is produced. Called Grandma Werling's Goetta, it is produced by Werling & Sons Inc., a fourth-generation meat company founded in 1886 by Joseph Werling. Grandma Werling is Eleanor George Werling, who was the backbone of the current company and daughter-in-law of the founder. Although it's really an Auglaize County grits recipe (without onions), USDA Standards of Identity prevent it from being can-labeled as grits, so it has to be labeled as goetta.

If you travel west of Auglaize County, Ohio, into Fort Wayne, Indiana, there is some residue of German grits, from its Germanic immigrant community, some of whom might have moved from the Auglaize County area.

Roger Franke of the Indiana German Heritage Society wrote in 2008:

In the past, German grits were very common to my home area near Ft. Wayne, Indiana. In a sense, it was the salvation of the family farm during the Depression in the 1930s. My father had purchased the 100 acre farm on which I grew up, from his father's estate in 1927, but by the early 1930s he ran into financial difficulties. He struck on the idea of butchering a hog almost every week during the cold months and peddling the butcher products in the German neighborhoods of Ft. Wayne. Though other butcher products were sold, the popularity of German grits was a significant factor in his sales intake. Today in Fort Wayne German grits are largely unknown.

HENRY COUNTY PRETTLES

If you travel farther north on I-75 from Minster, Ohio, and Auglaize County, you will hit Henry County. Napoleon, Ohio, is the epicenter of the Henry County prettles eaters. The area is in the northwest corner of Ohio, close to the Toledo metro area. It is known for its polka festivals. A large dance hall called the Bavarian Haus in Deschler hosts polka dances from February through May. Hamler, in Henry County, has an annual Summerfest in late July, when twenty-five-thousand people ascend to polka dance and eat sausages and prettles. Unlike its Eastern European neighbors to the east, in the Cleveland area, bratwurst and prettles are the dominant meat products, rather than kielbasa and pierogies. The area is mostly made up of descendants of north German Lutherans from a very specific area between Bremen and Munster called Visselhoevede.

While Goetta in Cincinnati and northern Kentucky is associated very much with the German Catholic population, in Henry County, prettles is associated with the Lutherans. There are over twenty Lutheran churches in Henry County and the surrounding area, most formed by small German immigrant farming communities in the late 1800s.

The first Lutheran families came with their faith when they left what was then the north German province of Hanover (now in the German state of Lower Saxony) to make their way to a place called Ohio in America. Little did they know that they'd be faced with densely forested, mosquito-infested, swampy land called the Black Swamp. But these German farmers were not discouraged. They saw familiarity with their lowland moor-surrounded villages in the fatherland. Through hard work they converted the swamp into some of the most productive farming lands in the state.

These first families came from the area around Visselhoevede, southeast of Bremen, in villages named Stellichte, Nindorf, Tietlingen, Fallingbostel, Ettenbostel, Hunsingen, Verdenermoor and Walsrode. The area that makes up this collection of villages, much like Henry County, was considered poor land, surrounded by eight marshy moors. The location was just west of the area called Luneburger Heath, which had its own gruetzwurst, called *heidiger knipp*, which used sheep meat instead of pork or beef.

The farm setup in this area of Germany was similar to serfdom. A *Meierhof* was a whole farm where the *Meier* was the estate administrator. He or she (an oldest daughter in a family of no sons could inherit the farm, and her husband would take her last name) had a number of dependent peasants who were obliged to pay taxes to him or her. The farm could include forests, garden mills, fish ponds, etcetera. There was an allotment of duties, so the *Halbmeier* was responsible for half of the farm duties, and the *Viertelmeier* was responsible for a quarter.

Farm numbers were allotted in the early 1600s in northern Germany, and no new farms were added or divided as families inherited the land. So, the farm was usually inherited by the oldest son or, in a case of a family with no sons, the oldest daughter. In the case of a daughter inheriting the land as Meier or Kolonus, her husband would take on her last name, an unusual practice in northern Europe. The other brothers and sisters had to find homes and other employment as adults, often having to get permission to marry from their oldest sibling, if they stayed on as tenant workers at the original family farm. In many cases, they did stay on at the family farm but took on other professions, like weaving or shoemaking, for extra money. Those who didn't like this servitude to the oldest sibling emigrated for better opportunity and freedom. That is also why many Germans were antislavery when they came to America in the time leading up to the Civil War. They had experienced that servitude, albeit in a much less brutal form.

Prettles, like Auglaize County grits, do not contain onions. The towns around Visselhoevede were surrounded by eight moors, and onions do not grow in swampy, marshy soil. Neunkirchen, where the Finkes were from, was right next to Visselhoevede, but the Finkes have always included onions in their goetta. This is probably because Neunkirchen-Voerden was outside of the moorlands.

The first settlement of these immigrants in Henry County was called New Hanover and centered on the Zion Church of New Hanover. Pastor August Knape from Germany was the first to minister to the newly arrived north German Lutherans of Henry County in the early 1850s. He organized services on the South Ridge in eastern Defiance County and the New Hanover settlement near what's now Napoleon in western Henry County.

In 1851, the original Church of New Hanover purchased property and built a log cabin on Henry County Road Q-1, a mile and a half west of St. Paul Lutheran Church in Napoleon Township. This is a half mile east of the Defiance/Henry County line. A cemetery on the site has many of the early immigrant pioneers and prettles eaters. It is now maintained by St. Paul, Napoleon Township.

The members of the New Hanover congregation lived around the nucleus of that church in both Defiance and Henry Counties. In the 1850s, when more emigrants were arriving from Germany, two new Lutheran churches in Adams Township were organized by residents of the Hanover Settlement.

After forming New Hanover, Pastor Knape continued to meet with other area families and developed the fledgling congregation, Bethlehem, near Okolona, in 1854, initially holding services in members' homes. The Bethlehem congregation grew and prospered. An examination of the confirmation records before 1871 reveals names of families still active over 150 years at Bethlehem, including Haase, Helberg, Helmke, Lange, Meyer, Norden, Prigge and Schroeder.

In 1882, the original Church of New Hanover disbanded, but its members continued to form other churches. The congregation folded into the St. Paul Lutheran Church in Napoleon and formed other churches, like "Hoffnung," or Hope Lutheran Church, in 1879 in Hamler, Ohio, by families from the Hanover Settlement who had started to move into the Hamler and Holgate areas in the 1860s.

German Lutherans in Henry County had to be trilingual. The first generation of young people had to learn to speak three languages: The Low German Plattdeutsch dialect their parents and grandparents brought with them, which was spoken at home; English at the required public school and also used for legal transactions; and High German Hochdeutsch for their German School (Summer School) lessons and catechism. German communion services were held during the year until the late 1960s or early 1970s. It was probably the hyperlocal Plattdeutsch dialect of the Visselhoevede area that the term *prettles* came from. Oddly enough, there is a grain sausage native to Kansas called pruttles that has the same "gedda" vs. "gudda" pronunciation difference that goetta has. So perhaps settlers of that area of Kansas are from the same area of Visselhoevede as the Henry County immigrants.

By the 1880s, Napoleon had more than three thousand residents. Like Minster to the south, Napoleon was a canal town. The population growth was due in part to the town's location on the Miami and Erie Canal and two separate railroad lines. At the time, most employment existed through businesses that made products for farmers in the surrounding countryside.

In 2001, a group of descendants of the original Henry County German immigrants met to organize a group to preserve their heritage. They formed the German Lutheran Heritage Society, which meets four times a year at the Lutheran Social Services building on State Route 66 near State Route 34. Another heritage group was formed around the same time called the Low German Club to preserve Plattdeutsch language understanding.

In December 2017, Roger Helberg of the German Lutheran Heritage Society and a descendant of the original 1848 Hanoverian immigrant

An image of the Miami and Erie Canal in Napoleon, Ohio. *Courtesy of Public Library of Cincinnati and Hamilton County.*

Christoph Heinrich Helberg (1833–1903), from the village of Ettenbostel (also members of the New Hanover community), gave a talk about his family making prettles at butcher time in the 1940s:

> *Butchering was family affair for the Helberg family even before I was born and continued into the 1950s. Dad would rent freezer space at the locker up town for steak, roast, and hamburger. Most of the other meat was canned or used to make sausage and prettles. The odd pieces and trimmings were ground up for summer sausage. Other trimmings were boiled with the pork trimmings from the pig butchering to be used for prettles. While the men made the sausage the women were boiling the trimmings from the beef and pork, about a 50/50 mix. The meat was removed from the kettle and pin oats were boiled in the broth. After the oats were tender, the ground beef and pork and oats was mixed with spices, salt and pepper and just a little bit of allspice. While it is still hot it was put in flat pans about two to three inches deep to cool. After everything was cleaned up and put away every family that helped was given a pan of prettles to take home.*

Herm's Meats in Napoleon on State Route 108 is the predominant maker of prettles in the area. Scott McMurtie is the third-generation owner, grandson of the founder, Herman Bischoff. Bischoff founded Herm's Sausage Shop in 1964 with old family recipes. He and his wife,

Helen Boesling Bischoff, had been making pork sausages on their twenty-acre farm near Okolona, Ohio, a German Lutheran hamlet between Napoleon and Defiance. Herm worked at a local meatpacking plant, where he learned the art of sausage making. He decided to turn his passion into a business.

Their main prettles recipe is Herm's, descended from his family, who were immigrants from the Visselhoevede area. The Bischoffs were members of the St. Paul Lutheran Church in Napoleon and the Bethlehem Lutheran Church in Okolona, as well as the Bavarian Haus in Deschler. That recipe has beef, beef heart, pin oats, salt, pepper and allspice. It is more similar to Cincinnati goetta than Minster grits and very similar to Westfalische Rindwurst, an all-beef grain sausage from that area. But the one key difference to goetta, which it shares with Auglaize County grits, is that there are no onions in the mix. According to Scott, there is a local prettles recipe that uses normal rolled oatmeal, which is also popular. In 2010, when Scott moved the business to Napoleon, he bought out Mohrings Carryout and took over its prettles recipe. That recipe has both pork and beef, with pinhead oats, salt, pepper and allspice. Between the two recipes, Scott says they make 125 pounds every two weeks.

If Herm's is the main meat market supplying prettles, then Spengler's Restaurant was the main place to eat prettles. It's the meeting place for all Napoleonites and the site of family and friend reunions. It resides in a beautiful 1892 Italianate building that housed the grocery in the front and a saloon in the back. It was founded by German immigrant brothers Wilhelm and Ernest Spengler, who descended from a long line of north Prussian farmers. They came over in the late 1860s with parents Wilhelm and Augusta Torre Spengler.

The building faced demolition in 1975 by then owners Community Bank, but 3,500 Henry County residents signed a petition against the plan, and the bank gave up its fight. Unfortunately, the current owners, the Weideman family, no longer serve prettles.

A former Spengler's owner, Fred Freppel, who took over in 1949, took pride in his prettles. A December 1973 *Toledo Blade* article memorialized his prettles with its title, "Prettles and Oats Are His Pride":

> *Bushel baskets filled with black walnuts, hickory nuts, and apples in front of Spengler's on Main Street in Napoleon, Ohio, were the first inklings that here is something special among grocery stores.*

Inside, the feeling of nostalgia continues and the first-time visitor is aware somebody really cares that the past is preserved in the present. That somebody is Fred Freppel who is known far and wide for a unique grocery store that boasts restaurant, just as unique located in the back of the store.

It wasn't easy, but well illustrates Mr. Freppel's determination to attain his goals in food merchandising. Prettles is a butchering-day meat, made of scraps of both pork and beef, seasoned with salt, pepper and allspice, and extended with steel-cut oats. The meat and seasonings were no problem, but steel-cut oats (as opposed to rolled oats) were not to be found in this part of the country. After letter writing and several telephone calls, Mr Freppel found them in Cedar Rapids, Iowa, and he now not only buys enough for his own prettles-making, but he also sells the oats by the pound.

The restaurant sings of the good old days. The booths and tables and chairs were purchased in 1933 and the back bar dates back to 1889. Mr. Freppel is up on his dates because he began working in the store in 1929 when it was operated by Ernest, Herman and William Spengler. He became owner in 1959. Ray Detterer has been cooking the restaurant foods since 1945, but when he is on vacation, Mrs. (Rozella) Freppel steps in to make some of her German specialties. One is baubalaspitule, which takes all day to prepare and cook. It is a sauerkraut and ham rolled in homemade noodle dough and cooked in the ham broth—a German version of pigs in a blanket.

As for the prettles, if you buy a pound, the directions are to fry it without shortening until it sticks, then turn it over and fry it until that side doesn't stick and keep it up until neither side sticks. Or you can let Mr. Freppel tell you himself.

Another place in Napoleon to eat prettles is Big G's Restaurant, where it's served as a choice of meat with eggs, and one truck stop about five miles out of town. But travel twenty miles in either direction from Napoleon and you won't find prettles.

Henry County residents like their prettles fried crispy. They also tend toward the sweet toppings rather than the savory. The most popular way to dress prettles, according to Scott McMurtie, is with molasses, although some slather jam on top or eat them plain on toast. Diane Elling, who has the blog "At the Riverbend" about Henry County German immigrants, said this about prettles: "I could never get these down. I think they are beef and pork remnants mixed with pinhead oats. They are browned and then at our house, some ate them on top of bread with strawberry jam. None of us kids liked them, as I remember."

There are still groups of folks in Henry County who get together and make huge batches of prettles in the fall. Jacobs Meats in Defiance, the former supplier to Spengler's Pub, also makes prettles, as does Brookview Farms in Napoleon, south of Archbold on Road 24, and the Holgate Market at 135 Railway Avenue.

Ohio's Germanic immigrants continue to carry on the traditions of their grain sausages carried over from northwestern Germany. However, grits are getting harer to find in Auglaize County, as are prettles in Henry County. Recipes have been perserved by both counties' historical societies, but neither has the advantage of the hype, marketing and Goettafest elevation that Cincinati does with goctta. So it's very important we perserve this legacy food trail in Ohio.

Chapter 10

BUTCHERS AND EARLY COMMERCIAL PRODUCERS

*P*art of what makes goetta unique and interesting are the small neighborhood butchers who make their own. Each butcher within a fifty-mile radius of downtown Cincinnati throws down with their own creative goetta flair, using different spice blends, some more aromatic and some more sweetly spiced. A recent trend has leaned toward spicier goettas, which the old Germans would certainly label as *sehr scharf* ("too spicy!"). But regional palates have changed since the Civil War, and millenials require more tickling of their taste buds. Some butchers play with the fattiness and recently have tried to make leaner, healthier goetta products. Others play with the ratio of beef to pork or meat to oats. Some use more onions than others. Some don't grind the meat or grate the onions as fine as others. A few have even taken the gutsy approach of developing turkey or vegan goettas. Whatever the differences, like our independent neighborhood chili parlors, Cincinnati goetta eaters are fiercely loyal to their favorite hometown butcher's goetta. And any Cincinnati butcher worth his trade makes his own goetta.

The local butchers supply their goetta to neighborhood church festivals and local high school sports stags.

Many meat markets and goetta store brands have come and gone, victims of big-box retailers and the changing landscape of American food. Ask any longterm Cincinnatian over the age of fifty, and you'll get a lament about the local butcher they grew up with and how much they miss their goetta or other products. Many of these butchers who have closed have shared their recipes with those still in business.

Mayor of Covington, Kentucky, from 1936 to 1939, Heinrich A. "Doc" Knollman was famous for his goetta, which he served in the 1930s and '40s at his meat market across from the former Bavarian Brewery. His father, Gerhardt Knollman, was an immigrant from Hoerstel, in the Steinfurt District of Westphalia, just to the west of Osnabruck in the Cradle of Goetta, so their recipe was probably very authentic.

The German Pioneer Verein (Club) stated that the first German butcher in Cincinnati was Jakob Boegele, but no mention is made as to whether or not he made goetta. A 1968 *Enquirer* article claimed that the first commercial producer of goetta in Cincinnati was the Adolph Sander Pork Packing Company of Gest Street in Cincinnati's West End. Adolph Sander was born in 1840 in Lenfoerge, Hanover, and came to Cincinnati in 1860, opening up a grocery on Clinton Street in 1865 and starting a pork-packing business with Louis Burkhardt in 1872, which he passed to his son Armin Sander after his death in 1912.

There is still a canned all-pork goetta product on the market, made in Burkettsville, Ohio, about ten miles due west of Minster, called Grandma Werling's Goetta. The company is a fourth-generation German meat company founded in 1886. Its goetta is not available in the Cincinnati area but can be ordered online. The family says that although it's based on the Minster-area grits, they must call it goetta, because the USDA has a definition only for goetta to which it can be USDA inspected.

Both Glier's and Queen City Sausage have said Dayton doesn't get goetta. Goetta sales fall off the cliff, according to Mark Balasa of Queen City Sausage, in Dayton as opposed to Cincinnati. Well, Dayton did get goetta at one time—it just forgot. The *Dayton Daily News* of the early 1950s advertised that Albers Supermarkets carried a Dutch Chef Brand of old-fashioned goetta. And Dot's Supermarkets of Dayton also carried Stegner's canned goetta in the mid- to late 1960s. There was even a Dayton beef-and pork-packing company, the Charles Sucher Company (founded by a Baden-Germany immigrant), which made a goetta under its Yummy Brand of meats in the mid-1960s. The company introduced it into the Cincinnati market through Kroger. Without the popular goettafests, appearances at local church festivals and restaurants and promotion among its butchers, what was once a thriving goetta market in Dayton died off.

Oddly enough, Columbus is a growing goetta market. Weiland's Gourmet Market in Clintonville sells Glier's goetta alongside Jones' scrapple. Thurn's Specialty Meats, Columbus' oldest butchery, founded in 1886, has made its own goetta recipe since the late 1980s, when one of its butchers left with its scrapple recipe. Thurn's goetta is beef and pork, spiced with marjoram, salt, pepper and onion powder. The company makes about five hundred pounds a year. A handful of restaurants in Columbus serve goetta as a breakfast meat. The former Diner in Powell used to serve goetta with the slogan, "The O is silent until you try it!"

Many greater Cincinnatians also assume that goetta is a West Side thing, because of its larger prevalence with local butchers there than on the East Side. But that's not true. Many East Side family butchers served their own housemade goetta. It's just that the West Side is better at preserving its heritage than the East Side.

Mairose Brothers Meats in Hyde Park at 3431 Monteith Avenue is one company that proves that goetta is not excluded from the East Side. The two Mairose brothers, Norbert A. and Arthur J., opened this small neighborhood meat market in 1938. It was taken over by their cousin Al Jackson in the 1960s, and then by his son Ken Jackson, who operated it until about 2014. It sold its own goetta made by the founders' mother, Laura Mairose, for many years.

Ed Bracke, of Bracke's Meats in Mount Lookout, said, "Anyone can make goetta if they just follow the recipe on the bag of Dorsel's pinhead oatmeal." Their business, which his father, a former butcher and Kroger manager, had founded in the late 1940s, closed around 2000. "Just stir the heck out of it!," Ed Bracke warned.

Many also remember Plaza Meats in Kenwood Plaza, which served homemade goetta from the 1950s to the '80s.

THE FORGOTTEN COMMERCIAL GOETTA BRANDS OF CINCINNATI'S PAST

Before the Glier family bought an old Bavarian Brewery building in 1967 and became the largest goetta manufacturer in the world, there were over a dozen other commercial goetta brands in greater Cincinnati that could be found at your local grocer's meat section.

Several things have happened leading to the demise of these brands. Many of the retail grocers where these products were offered (Dot's, Priceway, Parkview, Albers) are no longer around; the big retail chains like Kroger began the trend of gobbling up the small regional stores. Then there has been a shrinkage of local meat suppliers due to the large conglomerates like Sara Lee coming into retail and undercutting their pricing.

Today at Kroger there are only three brands of goetta that can be had. There's the two largest suppliers, Glier's and Queen City Sausage. And then there's our only commercially made vegan goetta, Jump N Joe's Grotta.

Kroger advertised its goetta in the *Cincinnati Times Star* as early as 1907. In the 1950s, Kroger made its own goetta under the Country Club store brand at the time. That brand even had a fictional Betty Crocker–like brand ambassador called Judith Anderson who even had her own radio show and cookbook series.

According to the Cincinnati Public Library, the first commercial producer of goetta was Sander Packing, which sold Morning Glory–branded meat products. German immigrant Adolph Sander, born in 1840 in Lenforge, Hannover, started the company in the 1870s. No doubt Sander's goetta recipe came from his Hanoverian roots. Sander came to the United States in 1860, starting work as a clerk at a grocery on Central Avenue. He was able to save and open his own grocery store. Then, he decided to partner with Louis Burckhardt and open a meatpacking plant on Gest Street, which developed into Sander Packing. Adolph Sander was a generous supporter of the Gerrman community and a member of many German organizations. He served as vice-president of the Cincinnati Zoological Gardens, was a major supporter of the German Theater Company and was a stockholder and director of the local German newspaper, the *Cincinnati Volksblatt*. The meatpacking business was passed on to Adolph's son Armin Sander, who taught a course at the University of Cincinnati on meatpacking house operations while operating the business until its closure in the late 1940s.

The USDA had made Standards of Identity for many meat products as a result of the early days of meat-making, as described in Upton Sinclair's *The Jungle*. By the mid-1960s, as federal inspectors saw that there were many regional meat products—many cousins of goetta—they came up with identity standards for them. As goetta was such a product being produced in large enough quantities by Glier's, H.H. Meyer and others, the USDA interviewed Bob Glier, founder of Glier's, about his recipe and used it to develop the federal standard, which defines goetta today. It states that goetta must contain 50 percent meat or meat by-products.

Many Cincinnati old-timers know Stegner's for its Cincinnati chili and mock turtle soup. The business was started near Findlay Market by Clarence Stegner in 1914. It made an all-pork goetta. In early December 1954, it made goetta history by being the first and only company to can goetta. Headlines in the *Cincinnati Enquirer* food section on December 9, 1954, proclaimed, "They've Canned Goetta and Jarred Frosting."

One of Cincinnati's favorite dishes, goetta, is now being offered in canned form by a well-known Cincinnati company. This will enable the homemaker to keep a supply on his or her pantry shelf, for it requires no refrigeration. To use it, cut both ends from the can and push it out.

The Stegner canned product made it through two label upgrades and into the mid-1980s, when Cincinnatians decided canned goetta was no longer acceptable. The company lasted four generations, to 2005. Also, flexible packaging technology had made it possible for one-pound tubes to be shelf stable. Apparently, canned goetta doesn't have the same appeal as canned cranberry jelly, which still remains on the shelves.

Before Jump N Joe went all-vegan, it had a very popular meat goetta that it sold around town. The company went all-vegan in 1965.

Several of the large meatpackers made their own goetta. With having the whole hog at their disposal, many of the meatpackers who slaughtered used their goetta product as a way to use up meat that would normally have been discarded. The 1985 Edward A. Kohl Company's goetta recipe, for example, called for pork cheeks from the head and pork skins, in addition to beef, oatmeal, onions, cereal, salt and spices. Lohrey's in Camp Washington had a goetta with its Brighton Belle line of meat and sausage products. The H.H. Meyer Packing Company made and marketed its own goetta in the late 1960s under the Partridge Brand meats. And Busch's sold its goetta at Thriftway, among other retailers, in the early 1960s.

Edelmann's at 2111 Kindel Avenue on the West End made its own goetta. Founded in 1930 by German sausage maker Martin Edelmann, it operated

An advertisement for Stegner's canned goetta. *Courtesy of Public Library of Cincinnati and Hamilton County.*

Stegner's Goetta

For easy-to-fix breakfast or a quick lunch! Delicious

15½-Oz. Can

39¢

The Bavarian Man logo of Edelmann, an early goetta producer. *Courtesy of Jim Kluener.*

into the 1980s, when Hoffman took over the Edelmann site. Hoffman's had its own Homemade brand goetta that it sold at retailers like Thriftway in the 1960s. Its goetta recipe was bought by Wassler's Meats and now is sold as Pop's Brand and as Homemade Goetta at Grayson's / Mike's Meats in Findlay Market.

There was also Dick Finke's Homemade Goetta, sold to local retailers like Remke Markets and restaurants in northern Kentucky. Black Angus shops made their own homemade brand of goetta as well in the 1960s.

TODAY'S PRODUCERS

Eckerlin

Eckerlin Meats at Findlay Market makes one of the most well-known local goettas. It produces about three hundred to five hundred pounds per week, and about one thousand pounds per week during the winter holidays. Eckerlin's Fine Goetta recipe is perhaps the oldest at Findlay Market. The founder of the business was Albert Eckerlin (1863–1937), who landed in the United States in 1890 from the Kingdom of Baden in Germany. Within a year of arriving, Albert had his own butcher shop near Findlay Market on West McMicken Street. He married Anna Maria Esslinger, also a Baden immigrant, in Cincinnati in 1892, and together they had six children, all future meat workers. By 1900, Albert had his own

ECKERLIN'S BEST

THE BEST GOETTA IN TOWN.

GOETTA

INGREDIENTS: Beef, Oatmeal, Pork, Beef & Pork Broth, Salt, Onions, Spices.

We would like to introduce you to one of the finest Goetta's on the market today. We have been making Goetta for over a century. A fine blend of spices and high quality pork & beef blend.

A SAVORY MIXTURE OF FRIED GOLDEN BROWN GOETTA IS PURE GERMAN HEAVEN.

KEEP REFRIGERATED

ECKERLIN MEATS
HISTORIC FINDLAY MARKET
1912 PLEASANT STREET BREEZEWAY
CINCINNATI, OHIO 45202
(513) 721-5743

Left: The label for Eckerlin's Best Goetta. *Courtesy of Eckerlin Meats.*

Below: The Eckerlin family at their Findlay Market meat counter. *Courtesy of Eckerlin Meats.*

slaughterhouse nestled into a tight residential area at the southwest corner of Clifton and Vine Streets. In 1909, the City Directory listed his slaughterhouse as a supplier of beef, fresh meats, sausages and provisions. He ran this until about 1910. He was a member of the German Pioneer Association in Cincinnati.

His sons Adolph (1905–1965) and Ernie (1903–1949) both established themselves as butchers, Adolph running a supermarket at 944 Hatch Street in Mount Adams where he made his own goetta. The Eckerlin's Best goetta label, used to package their goetta, has Adolph Eckerlin's photo in his store. Ernie Eckerlin ran a slaughterhouse at 1817 John Street

Frieda Eckerlin Lillis butchering meat at Finlay Market. *Courtesy of Public Library of Cincinnati and Hamilton County.*

in Cincinnati's West End until 1943, when wartime restrictions forced him to close. It was at Ernie Eckerlein's slaughterhouse that Elmer Hensler, the founder of Queen City Sausage, started his career in the meat business. Albert Eckerlin's oldest son, Emil (1901–1959), although he worked for his father at his shop, went on to work thirty years for mega-producer Kahn's in Camp Washington.

It was Albert's youngest daughter, Frieda Eckerlin Lillis, who ended up taking over the business at Findlay Market that he started in about 1890. She passed it on to her son Bob Lillis, who passed it on to his son Bob Jr. in 1983 at the young age of twenty-three. Today, Bob Jr. runs it with his children Christopher, Dan, Josh and Katie and his nephew Ryan. Eckerlin prides itself on only using quality cuts of meats, no scraps, in its goetta and making it in small batches. When I went for mine to taste, Josh Lillis, the fifth generation of the family, waited on me but didn't know the spice blend they use.

Their goetta is very lean and, as a result, needs butter to crisp in the pan as evenly as others. It is a bit crumbly as well. It has a nice flavor and a spice blend.

Stehlin Meat Market

If it wasn't for the 1913 flood, Stehlin Meat Market at 10134 Colerain Avenue in Bevis might not be around. And if it wasn't for the 1913 flood, we might not have one of the best goettas in Cincinnati and the last producer of a blood grain sausage. At the time, a young John "Butch" Stehlin was driving livestock by foot for his neighbor, German immigrant farmer Bill Espel. It was a twenty-mile round trip down US 27/Colerain Avenue from Dry Ridge to the Union Stockyards in Camp Washington and back. When the 1913 waters flooded the stockyards, Stehlin was stuck with livestock and ended up butchering them himself at Espel's barn off Colerain Avenue and selling the meat to his neighbors.

When I interviewed Dick Stehlin at the meat market one Saturday morning, I asked him where his grandfather got his goetta recipe. He gave an answer I had heard from other local Germanic butchers: "It was just a German recipe he [Butch Stehlin] got and modified." So that led me to search in the archives of St. James Church, where the Stehlins were members. Here I found the wedding photo of the daughter of Bill Espel, Mary Espel, and her husband, Harry Kleine. I noticed her wedding veil in the picture. It had a very tall and ornate headdress that looked like the large *kranzmaikes*, the wedding headdresses of women from the Hanover region of Germany, that I had seen in photos. They're very showy and almost like that of a Las Vegas showgirl. This regional headdress is like a round hatbox covered in multicolor beads or baubles. Like Hanoverian brides, Mary Espel was also wearing a wide-flairing, high collar in this photo. So, through census records, I was able to verify that her father, Bill Espel, was indeed an immigrant from Hanover.

So how does that connect to Butch Stehlin, an Alsatian immigrant, and his goetta recipe? Well, his first slaughtering in the year of the great flood was in Hanoverian immigrant Bill Espel's barn. Of course, a man from Hanover, familiar with grain sausages from his motherland made at the time of slaughter, would have shown Stehlin how to make goetta, a way to use all parts of the pig and cow. What a great way to improve the profits from slaughter. Stehlin probably modified and perfected this recipe to his likes and operations. Thus, Stehlin goetta was born.

John's father, Joseph Stehlin, was a farmer in Bevis in the Germanic immigrant Catholic farming community around St. John the Baptist Catholic Church on Dry Ridge Road. The church was and still is a very important part of the lives of the Stehlin family. John and Eleanora Stehlin donated an organ and a piano to the church. You can understand why immigrant farmers settled in this beautiful nook of Hamilton County if you drive along Dry Ridge Road from busy Colerain Avenue. The hills and vistas of the Great Miami Valley are stunning. You can almost hear the mooing of cattle grazing on Owl's Creek. Some of the original farmhouses still stand from those early days, and the final resting place of many of those families at St. John the Baptist Cemetery are noted in German. John's grandfather Martin Stehlin had immigrated to Cincinnati from Alsace-Lorraine in the 1840s. Bill Espel, John's first employer, had immigrated to Cincinnati in 1880 from the Kingdom of Hannover, in the Cradle of Goetta. The sharing of goetta recipes from Cradle of Goetta immigrants to Germanic immigrants from other regions happened all across greater Cincinnati and northern Kentucky.

The legacy of butchering in-house has stayed with the business for over one hundred years. Their livestock comes from third- and fourth-generation farmers in the surrounding areas of Shandon, Ross, Hamilton and Cedar Grove. So Stehlin's goetta is hyperlocal. You could even say that it's Colerain Township Goetta. That is, except for the pinhead oats they use, which come from North College Hill Bakery. The bakery buys pinhead oats in bulk for

John Stehlin and his wife, Eleanora, in 1920. *Courtesy of Stehlin's.*

The original Stehlin Smokehouse. *Courtesy of Stehlin's.*

itself and several other butchers who make goetta in Cincinnati. You can even buy a Stehlin house brand of pinhead oats, supplied by North College Hill Bakery, which has a huge rack in the Stehlin store fully stocked with its delicious baked goods.

John went off to fight in World War I with his business barely off the ground. On returning with a severe case of trench foot, he married his sweetheart, Eleanora Wullenweber, in 1920 and, with her, started a family of two daughters and three sons—Vernon, Ervan and Harold— who grew up with the business. A sausage house behind the store is where he developed his recipes for pork sausage, liver pudding, goetta, headcheese and Johnny-in-the-Bag, a local blood sausage and cousin of goetta. Although hundreds of butchers used to make Johnny-in-the-Bag in Cincinnati, Stehlin's is the only one that still makes it, which it does seasonally between October and May.

In 1946, with help from his brother, Butch built his own slaughterhouse behind the store. Prior to that, he used a house in Camp Washington and hauled the cut pork, beef and sheep back to his store in Bevis. It used to be a tradition that whenever you opened a new store or started something new, you asked the church pastor to bless it. So the Stehlins asked Father Kuntz, pastor of their church, St. John the Baptist, to kill the first bullock. Their first load of hogs to be butchered was provided by Oscar Steiner.

They survived the Depression, a near relocation due to Interstate 275 and the onslaught of retail chain competition, and they are now into the fourth generation. The grandsons became stockholders in 1988. All worked at Stehlin's through grade school and high school. Ervan's sons Ken, Ron and Dick, and Harold's sons Denny and John all became full-time employees after graduating from high school. Denny and Dick took up major roles in slaughtering and processing. Ron took on meat truck duty and later freezer beef processing, while John took over running the store.

Saturday mornings are busy at the store, and you definitely need to take a number as soon as you walk in. A reclining hog bench greets you at the front entrance to the store, just in case you need to take a break. Customers inside discuss the best cut of meat with the butchers to have for their meals. The Stehlins are dedicated to their service, but if you get any of them talking, you'll hear stories about Sister Charles, a nun at Saint John the Baptist who put Denny in a headlock, or Father Kuntz's unsuccessful try at grinding beef for the store and getting a scolding by Butch.

Dick Stehlin says they spice their goetta with only salt and pepper—no bay leaf, nutmeg or allspice. But the freshness of their meat makes all the difference in its flavor. Stehlin puts a little head meat in its goetta, which is similar to how Minster grits and prettles are made. And frankly, this is probably more authentic to the original version that came over with the immigrants, a sign that this producer of goetta actually slaughters its own livestock and has the other parts available. Its goetta does have a great flavor, and the grind of meat is not as fine as others, but it creates a creamier version that crisps fantastically when fried. From October through April, the Stehlins make over three hundred pounds of goetta a week. During the slower summer months, they make about two hundred pounds. Recently, they've made a spicy goetta with red pepper and a jalapeño goetta, both of which are becoming very popular with their customers.

Sign commemorating the first bullock killed by Father Kuntz of St. John Dry Ridge Catholic Church. *Courtesy of Stehlin.*

Although they've had a food booth at St. John Dry Ridge's summer festival for decades, 2017 was the first time they supplied goetta. Like many other butchers, they've shared recipes with their friends in the business. Mark Edelmann of Edelmann Company was friends with John Stehlin, so he shared a lot of his sausage recipes. And, when Clifton Meats closed, owner Paul Jaeger came to work for the Stehlins and used his Cincinnati brat and mett recipes. The Stehlins' commitment to quality and service is evidenced by their longtime employees and the generational loyalty of their customer base.

Avril Bleh & Sons

Avril Bleh is one of the oldest continually operating butcher shops in Cincinnati, at 33 East Court Street. It has been a Cincinnati staple since 1894, when Anton Avril, an immigrant from a long line of butchers in Geinsheim, Palatinate, Germany, started selling his smoked meats out of a wagon at Findlay and Court Street Markets. Anton built the business into such a success that he was given the title "The Cincinnati Ham King." He passed it to his oldest son, Ferdy, who passed it along to his two sons Fred and Werneth, who operated it until 1998. That's the year Len Bleh bought the shop, adding his own name to the family-owned legacy. The butchery had been at the Court Street shop since 1926, which at the time was at the Court Street Market and saw lots of pedestrians.

Friends thought Len Bleh was nuts for buying the shop from the Avril brothers in the distressed Court Street area, but he has developed a name for himself among Cincinnatians, and the area has grown with businesses and restaurants. And now, with the new downtown Kroger being built nearly next door, he looks forward to even more foot traffic to his butchery. Although he kept the one-hundred-year-old Boss mixer used to finely grind the pork for Cincinnati brats, Len spent a great deal of money upgrading the equipment and facilities, including adding capacity to the smokehouse.

Avril Bleh & Sons has been voted best butcher by *Cincinnati Magazine* and has almost a cult following. They provide sausages to local restaurants, like the Senate in nearby Over-the-Rhine. And they offer one of the coolest opportunities in Cincinnati to learn the sausage makers' art. Len and his son host a Sausage University all-day course, in which a dozen lucky laymen and -women can get a peek and learn how to make about a dozen different

An early Avril advertisement. *Courtesy of Public Library of Cincinnati and Hamilton County.*

sausages. I happen to be a 2016 graduate of that course. Unfortunately, there is not enough time to learn how to make their goetta.

Ferd Avril made goetta in oatmeal sausage–linked form and didn't add onions, because he didn't like them. His sons finally added onions, but not a lot, to the mixture in the 1970s, probably at the urging of customers. Today, Avril & Sons makes goetta with and without onion. The meat is more shredded than ground, like many older recipes. It is also one of the few butchers that still makes the old-fashioned smoked, linked version of goetta called "oatmeal rings" and liver pudding, which is similar to the livermush of the Carolinas.

Werneth Avril, the third-generation owner of Avrils, passed away in September 2018 in Dallas, Texas, where he had retired after selling the business. But his family's legacy lives on through Len Bleh and his son.

Wassler Meats

Wassler Meats has been selling its goetta from its current store, at a strip mall at 4300 Harrison Avenue, since 1970. It makes a brand it calls Pop's Homemade Goetta, which is the old Hoffman-recipe goetta. Wassler Meats offers a regular and a hot goetta, of which it makes about four hundred pounds a day, except Sundays, when it is closed.

Eugene "Pop" Wassler came to Cincinnati from Alsace-Loraine in 1880 at the age of fourteen. His brother Edmund hosted him until he married Minnie Sporle, from Stuttgart, Germany. After the birth of his son Fred in 1894, with an investment of fifty dollars, Pop opened his first store at the corner of Wade and Denman Streets in Cincinnati's West End neighborhood, where most of his customers spoke German. He moved a couple of times, ending up in Over-the-Rhine at Liberty and Sycamore, then at Fourteenth and Republic, and for a time, the family had a second store at Findlay Market from 1930 to 2001. In 1970, they moved the anchor store to the West Side.

Pop's son Fred took over the business in 1930 and never retired, working at the West Side store until his death in 1985 at ninety-one. He drove Wassler's first delivery truck, a 1913 Model T Ford, and was president of the Cincinnati Retail Meat Dealer's Association. Fred's sons Gene and Bob continued to run the market, and now the fourth generation, brothers Kenny and David Wassler, operate the business with their sons Michael and Chris. The family rule was that as soon as you were tall enough to see over the counter, you went to work in the store. They've learned a couple of things in their days. They always eat standing up. And a Wassler could never do anything important on a Saturday—like get married or have a baby—because it's the busiest day of the week.

Like Eckerlin's at Findlay, Wassler's Meats sells bakery products from another longtime family-owned business, North College Hill Bakery. It's a

An advertisement for Wassler's goetta, showing the logo of Pop Wassler holding his butcher knife. *Courtesy of Wassler Meats.*

perfect marriage; you can get a delicious roll of cinnamon bread made by NCH to go with your goetta and eggs for Sunday breakfast.

In addition to their goetta recipe, there's another interesting artifact passed down through the Wassler generations. A muzzle-loading rifle from 1801, owned by Landelin Wassler, the grandfather of the founder, in Alsace-Lorraine, has been passed down for at least six generations.

Fourth-generation owners, brothers Ken and Dave Wassler, still enjoy coming into work every day. And soon-to-be fifth-generation employess, brothers Mike and Chris, Ken's sons, are proud of their family's nearly 125-year-old meat legacy.

Bridgetown Finer Meats

In a strip mall at 6135 Bridgetwon Road, owners Richard Hoehn, Brian Brogan, Mark Bender, Rob Bleh and Mike Fickinger run a busy meat and produce shop. The shop opened to West Siders in 1979 and has been dedicated to bringing the finest-quality meats since then. The store is filled with lots of energy. The boys handle the meat side, and the girls tend to the produce and grocery side of things. The shop makes a very lean, all-pork goetta that is very oats-and-onion forward with mild flavor. It also makes a turkey goetta for those looking for an alternative to red meat.

Hammann's Meats & Catering

Hammann's is nestled in a valley on Old Winton Road in the northwest Cincinnati neighborhood of Pleasant Run Farms, at the border of Hamilton and Butler Counties. My parents have been patronizing the meat market there since it opened. Grandpa Hammann (class of '63) graduated only a few years after my father from Roger Bacon High School. The large mobile smoker parked alongside the shop is a clue to the amount of meat they smoke for their catering business. It's a well-provisioned butcher and grocery, and you're greeted as soon as you walk in by the husky Rob Hamman or one of his friendly staff.

They spice their Grandpa Hammann's Homemade Goetta with the aromatics garlic and ginger, along with the typical salt, pepper and nutmeg. It has a very aromatic flavor, very different from most goettas. Making about 150 pounds per week (three batches of eighteen-loaf pans), it is the unofficial goetta of the Germania Society Annual Oktoberfest, only a few miles west on John Gray Road. Hammann's goetta and rye sandwiches are among the great Germanic foods that fuel the wildly popular Germania Oktoberfest Sunday tug-of-wars, which Rob Hamman has chaired. It usually ends in a bitter duel between Springfield Township firemen and policemen. Hammann's also supplies goetta to St. Gabriel's Summer Festival and the Elder West of the Rhine and Wine summer beergarden event.

The business was founded in June 1991 at 1369 Compton Road in Mount Healthy, Ohio, by John and Pat Hammann, along with their sons. Their American dream has resulted in nearly twenty-five years of successful business in the retail meat, deli and catering business. John was nearing middle age, having worked at the beloved Edelmann Sausage Company in the West End—where their goetta recipe comes from—and the meat business for thirty years. So it was a natural progression for someone with drive. The first store on Compton Road was primarily a retail business, run by John, with help from sons Ryan and Rob.

At that time, catering was not the large portion of their business that it is today. Today, you can get their homemade goetta in the Homestyle Breakfast Buffet catering package. In addition to wedding catering packages, they have an awesome Taste of Germany package that is unparalleled in Cincinnati. By the mid-1990s, with the substantial increase in business, relocation became necessary, due to the lack of expansion possibilities at the Compton Road location. So they opened a newly remodeled, twenty-five-hundred-square-foot facility at 7864 Hamilton Avenue in Mount Healthy. Hammann's thrived at this prime location with plenty of exposure, ample parking and additional amenities, such as beer, wine, tobacco, lottery and groceries. With the tremendous exposure and added convenience, the business became well established.

The Hammann family, John, Pat, Rob, Ryan and Jason, continued to run the business with old-fashioned butcher-shop flare and friendly service. In

Above: Rob Hamman making goetta at Germania Park Oktoberfest. *Image courtesy of Hammann.*

Left: This is the Homemade brand goetta that Hammann's Meats produces in about 150 pounds a week. *Author's collection.*

September 1999, Rob opened the family's second location at 6180 Winton Road, Pleasant Run Farms. This three-thousand-square-foot facility is only about five miles north of the Mount Healthy location. So when they decided to close the Mount Healthy store in March 2001, it wasn't too hard for their existing customers to still patronize the business. A nonrenewable lease at the Mount Healthy store and the mega-opportunities for catering in Fairfield and Butler Counties made this a bittersweet but easy decision. Apparently, the owners were wanting to sell the property to a big-box retailer, which they did the next year. This national trend by community leaders wanting to cash in has been at the expense of small, hometown, family-owned businesses.

Hammann's has grown to fifteen employees, providing services for its customers as well as offering many new items, like their homemade dry rubs and barbecue sauces. John, Rob and family, along with their dedicated staff, plan to continue to serve the Fairfield, Pleasant Run, Mount Healthy and surrounding areas for years to come with their trademark friendly approach and quality products.

Like several other local butchers, they support family-owned businesses by supplying baked goods from the North College Hill Bakery. To show their appreciation for customers, they're very involved in the community, supporting Fairfield City Schools and the Joe Nuxall Miracle League and providing the meats for the St. John Neuman Pig Roast, up the hill from their shop on Old Winton/Mill Road.

R & R Quality meats

R & R Quality Meats at 4029 Harrison Avenue has been serving and singing to the West Side neighborhood of Cheviot since 1963. Owned by Bob Thomas, it makes a turkey goetta and regular homemade goetta. Its catering business, which serves the Lasalle High School Sports Stag every year, can handle upward of one-thousand-person events.

Langen Meats

In the West Side neighborhood of White Oak at 5585 Cheviot Road is the oldest of the three stores that third-generation owners, brothers Greg and Jim Langen, run with their partner, Nick Ruther.

Image of 1920s Mohawk store with Harry Langen and Jimmy Wind behind the counter. *Courtesy of Greg Langen.*

Greg and Jim's grandfather Harry J. Langen opened the first retail meat store in the downtown neighborhood of Mohawk in 1924. Growing up with five other siblings on Liberty Street in Cincinnati's Over-the-Rhine, Harry helped his younger brother Elmer break into the retail meat business. Elmer would be a founding member of the greater Cincinnati Meat Dealer's Association and own three stores himself. Their father, Johann Heinrich Langen Jr., was a horseshoer at a blacksmith shop in Over-the-Rhine, as was their grandfather Johann Heinrich Sr., who emigrated from Germany to Cincinnati in 1845.

There's a town called Langen in Lower Saxony, near Oldenburg, right in the middle of the Cradle of Goetta in Germany.

The family chose to open a second store in White Oak in 1959, and they closed the Mohawk store two years later. In 1981, they opened the Harrison, Ohio store at 1170 Harrison Avenue, and in 1987, they opened a shop in Batesville, Indiana, at 215 East Pearl Street. Although goetta sells pretty well in Batesville, with its strong Germanic population, it doesn't sell as well as in the Cincinnati stores.

Langen stocks a variety of products, including North College Hill Bakery's products. If you want to get there before the Saturday morning rush, you'll need to arrive before 10:00 a.m. At least seven friendly butchers are on-site helping customers, cutting meats and making or portioning goetta. Greg and the others know most of their customers by name and ask how the rest of their family is doing. To waste none of the pork, they even offer fresh pig ears for the family dog.

Langen's goetta recipe is that of the founder, Harry J. Langen—an all-pork, warmly spiced one. Greg pronounces it "gutta," the old-school way, so you know their goetta is authentic. He won't reveal the secret blend of spices they use, which only three people know, but he does say they get their pinhead oats in bulk from BakeMark Products in Fairfield, Ohio. When asked to compare it to Glier's, he says it's leaner—they use only pork shoulder—and has more flavor, with deeper spicing. Between the three stores, they make about five hundred pounds of it a week for loyal West Side customers. How does Greg Langen like to dress his goetta? He replies emphatically: "No dressing at all. That would insult my gutta!" Greg says his goetta customers span all ages, but the younger ones are usually from goetta families who are already familiar with it. In addition to the original Grandpa Langen goetta, they make an all-turkey goetta, a hot goetta and a bacon goetta with finely

The variety of goetta products at Langen Meats in White Oak. *Author's collection.*

chopped bacon, giving it "the best of both worlds," as Greg explains. They have even added a goetta cream gravy that one of their butchers developed. It goes great with biscuits and on tater tots.

Langen Meats is also known for something else: its smoked potatoes. Greg says that, after you've had a smoked potato, you won't want them any other way. It's a hyperlocal delicacy many Cincinnati butchers used to offer, but as far as Greg knows, he's the only one still doing it in town. It takes a special, expensive piece of equipment that pressure cooks and smokes at the same time. Goetta and smoked potato home fries sounds like a yummy breakfast!

Humbert's Meats

Jim Humbert and his wife, Barbara, West Side residents, opened their first meat market at Glemore Avenue and Werk Road in 1964. Over the next fifteen years, he built a meat empire of four more stores throughout the Cincinnati metro area. Three of his four children went on to work for Humbert's operations full-time. In 1979, Humbert branched out of retail food sales and opened HMI Distributors, a distribution company, and then started Cincinnati Gourmet Meats, which produced a variety of items, including honey-glazed hams and corned beef. Due to the growth of HMI Distributors, Humbert eventually sold each of the locations to the store managers, who now run the operations.

Brothers Mike and Scott Daubenmerkl own Humbert's Meats at 9211 Winton Road in Finneytown, which they took over from their father, George. Both are graduates of Elder High School but employ graduates of other area schools, like Roger Bacon. They make a turkey and a regular goetta.

Brothers Boone and Pat Murray co-owned the West Side locations. Pat manages the Rapid Run Drive site, and Boone operates the Bridgetown Road location. Don Murray owns the Bridgetown store

J.B.'s Barbecue Pit in Elsmere, Kentucky

Located at 133 Garvey Avenue in Elsmere, Kentucky, J.B.'s Barbecue has been servicing the greater Cincinnati and tri-state area with their quality products for over forty-four years. Founded by John Baxter Sr. in 1974, J.B.'s has a long history with the meat business, which includes working for Kroger and several other independent markets. In February 2007, John

Baxter Jr. sold the company to Randy and Kathleen Guilfoyle. The couple is committed to carrying on the high quality of goetta set by Baxter and expanding into a greater portion of the retail and catering sector.

At its USDA-inspected plant, J.B.'s produces a wide variety of delicious products. From its All Natural Pulled Pork Bar-B-Q and Western Style sauce to its Homemade Goetta, Shredded Beef, Tasty Shredded Pork, Thick Old Style Chili, Pulled Beef and Famous Kentucky Pig Roast, J.B.'s has the meats for your event.

The Hitching Post Restaurant in Hyde Park is one of many in greater Cincinnati that uses J.B.'s goetta. It serves J.B.'s with eggs, alongside its famous Kettle Kakes, a sort of midwestern beignet. J.B.'s goetta is described as having a creamy texture, simliar to Stehlin's goetta. This appeals to those who prefer a chunkier meat over a finely ground meat consistency.

Gramma Debbie's

Debbie Knueven Gannaway, owner of Gramma Debbie's at Findlay Market, grew up on goetta. She pronouces it the right way, "gutta." She says whenever someone comes to her stall and pronouces it that way, she "wants to grab and kiss 'em." Her paternal grandmother, who came from northern Germany, taught her father how to make goetta, and he taught his wife, Debbie's mother.

In addition to a "slightly spicy" beef and pork goetta, she sells a vegan goetta, made with pinhead oats, tofu, quinoa and flax seeds, with no meat, no dairy and no gluten. She spices her goetta with white pepper, cloves, nutmeg and cayenne pepper.

In 2016, while in town playing Felix in *The Odd Couple* at the Aronoff Center, vegetarian actor Thomas Lennon, famous for playing Jim Dangle in *Reno 911!*, bought Gramma Debbie's vegan goetta and loved it. Now that's a resounding testimonial!

VEGAN GOETTA: WHAT THE HECK?

A member of my Facebook group "Cincinnati's Oldest Goetta Recipe" posted a while ago, "So I just tried vegan goetta." This sparked a nearly viral chain of responses. People said things like, "That's just blasphemy,"

Gramma
Debbie's
Kitchen
Gluten
Free!

Vegan
GOETTA

Pinhead Oats, Tofu,
Quinoa, Flax Seeds
No Meat, No Dairy, No Gluten
Seasoned with
White Pepper, Cloves, Nutmeg,
Touch of Cayenne

$4.99 per lb.

Grandma Debbie's goetta at
Findlay Market. *Author's collection.*

"There's no such thing," "That's just a fried oat cake" and "I'm sorry, that's just wrong." So there are fairly strong opinions against vegan goetta in the goetta-eating community.

For a meat product like goetta that has an inherent sausage envy and wants more meat content, why in the world would anyone want to make it vegan? Vegan scrapple is just polenta. Then what is vegan goetta? Mother's oats? Well, in vegan goetta's defense, we have amped up the quality of meats used in goetta since it was introduced. We use pork shoulder instead of head parts and other less-appetizing bits of the pig and cattle. Why not amp it up a bit more on the healthy scale and just flavor it like meat, but use nonmeat products? That's what a growing number of goetta producers in greater Cincinnati have been doing recently. It just goes to show our love for goetta. The fact that a native who decides to go vegan for health or other reasons would experiment and go to the trouble to create a vegan goetta product shows how much we crave the flavor and experience of eating goetta.

Jump N Joe Grotta is the only commerically produced and available vegan goetta on the market. It's both the brand and the name of the company. Jump N Joe has been in business since 1952 in Cincinnati.

Jump N Joe's Grotta, a vegan product made since 1965. *Author's collection.*

Originally, along with a very popular goetta, it also had a full line of meat products, like Cincinnati chili, barbecue and regular chili, as well as deli salads like German and regular potato salads and slaw. The company sold its goetta and other products within greater Cincinnati from northern Kentucky to Wilmington, Ohio, which may have been the farthest reach of goetta up to that time. At the time, goetta was a winter-only product. Jump N Joe was brilliant in the mid-1950s for trying to extend the goetta season into spring by marketing it, in a city with a lot of German Catholics, as "the ideal Lenten food for any meal."

In 1965, Jump N Joe, way ahead of its time, decided to take out the meat and supply only Grotta, a vegan goetta product. This was right about the time that the USDA put a great deal more regulation on meat-product companies. So the removal of meat made its production less expensive and certainly less regulated. The company's decades of collective knowledge and experience gave it a unique advantage in providing a healthy product, which is how it promotes the product.

Today, the product is sold in one-pound tubes like Glier's and Queen City meats and is made in a factory in Batavia. It contains both pinhead oats and cornmeal. The company has sold it to health-food stores, as well as to Kroger groceries. It promotes the soluble fiber as reducing cholesterol and maintaining steady blood-sugar levels, which is good for keeping your appetite in check and preventing diabetes. Jump N Joe also promotes it as a vegetarian product and good for dieting, with only sixty calories per serving.

I remember as a kid in the 1980s my dad bringing home Jump N Joe Grotta for us to try. We thought, "goetta, without the meat. It sounds a lot like just fried Cream of Wheat!" The only difference is that grotta contains cornmeal in addition to pinhead oats, which is not in goetta, and thus gives it a different, mealy texture than most goetta afficianados would expect. It also kind of makes it more like a savory polenta. For us, it was just too outside of our box. We demanded meat in our goetta, so no more Grotta for the Woellerts. But, the longevity of Jump N Joe's Grotta is a testimony of its popularity in Cincinnati.

In the last several years, with the growing trend of healthier eating and those who decide to live the vegetarian lifestyle, many local producers have come out with vegan and vegetarian versions. A popular restaurant in the Northside neighborhood, Honey's, which operated from 2005 to 2013, had a vegan goetta created by Chef Shoshanna Haffner that I liked a lot. Paired with its famous Binkle fries and spicy chili sauce, this made for an incredible breakfast.

A group of 1950s Dayton High School students hanging out in front of a sign for Jump N Joe's Goetta. *Courtesy of Old Photos of Cincinnati.*

The former owner of Melt, Lisa Kagan, had a version that she served at the restaurant and at her small grocery, Picnic and Pantry. Vegan Roots owner Caitlyn Bertsch has a version she likes to make, which can be ordered at the Brewhouse in Walnut Hills and at Bella Vino in West Chester. The popular vegan café Park + Vine, in Over-the-Rhine, owned by Danny Korman, was one of the few places in greater Cincinnati where vegan goetta was regularly served.

The challenge with creating a vegan goetta is getting it to stay together in a slice and not crumble apart. While making it, the cook must get the moisture content right so that it stays together when sliced, and so that it fries up crispy without the fat. Some vegetarian versions use mushrooms as the base, while others use tofu and other grains like flaxseed and quinioa, along with pinhead oatmeal.

Several suppliers have taken a half step into healthier goetta by offering turkey goetta. Langen Meats, Glier's and Bridgetown Finer Meats all have versions of turkey goetta.

Thankfully, there have been no experiments into exotic meat goetta, or seafood goetta, but Cincinnatians of varying health regimes go to great lengths to get that taste of goetta that meets their needs.

There are many local butchers in Cincinnati and Northern Kentucky not mentioned here who make goetta. And that's the brilliant thing about it all. There are always new chefs, butchers and restaurants making goetta and putting their own character into it. While many of the forms would not be at all familiar to the Germanic immigrants who brought it to the area, they certainly keep this historic comfort food alive and evolving with new tastes and lifestyles. And goetta is a lifestyle, certainly for those of us who love and cherish it. I hope I have helped you goetta life.

Chapter 11

GOETTA RECIPE REDUX

G oetta has come a long way since it first arrived. And I've learned from my Facebook page "Cincinnati's Oldest Goetta Recipe" that there are hundreds, maybe thousands, of variations on goetta. Types and cuts of meat vary, as do the spices, the cooking method and the use of onions. Some variations to original recipes have happened because of the cooking method changing, the ingredients not being available, an evolution of flavors to spicier levels and modifications because of health.

Think how much cooking appliances have changed since the coal- and wood-fired ovens in which goetta was first made by the Germanic immigrants. Maybe the only appliance that is the same today as it was for the original immigrants is the cast-iron skillet, which perfectly crisps slices of goetta. Ovens have gone gas, then electric, then induction and now back to gas. We've had help from other inventions, like the pressure cooker, the microwave, the Crock-Pot, and now the Instapot and air fryer. Grills have come a long way, too, and we now have linked and patty products that are grillable. Packaging and refrigeration have come a long way, from the ceramic crock to the first shelf-stable heat shrink packaging, and from iceboxes to smart refrigerators. Goetta is no longer a winter-only product.

But what ingredients does goetta have to include to really be considered goetta? It has to have both beef and pork. It must include white onions. Of course it must use pinhead oats, steel cut oats or any unrolled oats. It must include mild savory spices, salt and pepper. But just these handful of simple ingredients can create unfathomable variations.

Starting with the meats, most goetta recipes call for a one-to-one ratio of pork and beef. A standard-size batch uses one pound of each. My maternal great grandmother used a pound of pork flank, a fattier cut on the belly of the pig between the ribs and hind legs. My maternal grandmother's sister's mother-in-law used a pound of pork neck. Numerous recipes printed in the *Cincinnati Enquirer* reference using pork neck bones for better flavor. The 2018 *Germania Society Cookbook* has a very old goetta recipe from Elsie Doscher, the former owner of Doscher Candy Company. It is a pork-only goetta, which calls for four pounds of pork neck bones and describes the labor in using them: "Pick meat from the neck bones. Discard any gristle or very dark meat that might be between bones. Go through meat very carefully with your fingers to be sure all small bones are sifted out."

Stehlin's Meats uses a bit of pork cheek in its goetta, which is very original, as most early grain sausage recipes used the head meat. And commercial producer Glier's uses pork hearts and skin in its goetta. The fatty skin helps to congeal the final product and also helps it fry crispy in the pan.

Because our grain sausage, goetta, was a city product, and in a city that was known for its livestock businesses, ours quickly evolved to use better cuts of meat than, say, the head meat, organs or less-desirable cuts, than the gritswurst of the American Midwest. Cincinnati butchers always separated out the grain sausage that used liver, calling it liver pudding, which is an indication that goetta, unlike other related grain sausages like boudin, jitrnice and others, never included liver or other organs.

Most goetta producers use a pork cut called the callie cut, the picnic cut or the pork butt—all of which are actually parts of the pig shoulder. And most use ground beef or ground chuck. Some even take the grinding piece out and use ground pork sausage in the tube. Many even use a spicy pork sausage for more flavor. Those looking for a different and even spicer option might try adding an amount of pork chorizo sausage. I haven't seen that on any recipes, as it is more Latin than German, but I think it's worth a try. Another new variation I saw was using Bavarian bratwurst, or weisswurst, out of the casing as part of the pork. That would add parsley to the flavoring, which is a standard ingredient in Bavarian weisswurst. I'm not sure it is a proper herb for goetta.

A friend of mine, John K., who is an avid smoker, thought that using ground smoked meat would offer a different flavor to goetta. I know that some of the early butchers in Cincinnati would smoke oatmeal rings, or goetta in sausage form. I wonder if smoking the meat loses some of the liquidy fat needed to help congeal in the loaf pans. I have seen a recipe that adds a drop of liquid smoke to the oatmeal cooking liquid.

There are commercial versions of turkey goetta, for those wanting a leaner meat. However, I've tried some of these products from the variety of meat markets, and I just don't think they offer the same flavor as beef and pork do. It tastes like a completely different product. A lot of locals who are deer hunters make venison goetta. Finke's is the only meat market that offers a venison goetta. Venison is extremely lean, and, as in venison chili, a fattier meat like ground beef would have to be added to the venison to make a good goetta, in my opinion. I have not tried a venison product. However, I have tried Fond Restaurant's all-sheep goetta and found it very good.

Whatever meat is used, there is a debate as to how fine to grind the meat. Some people like a chunkier goetta, while others, like myself, prefer a more fine-ground meat. The meat should be cooked first, in water, and drained from the stock to cook the oats. For oventop cooking, three cups of liquid to each pound of meat should be used. If there is not enough stock, the three cups should be supplemented with water to make up three cups per pound. If the meat is already ground, you can use canned beef and pork stock or boullion, but homemade stock is always better. If you use a Crock-Pot, about a cup less water is needed of a six-cup oventop batch. Even less water, about half of the oventop version, is needed in an Instapot. The end result is a cooked goetta that is not too runny when you put it in the loaf pans; otherwise, it will not congeal to a proper consistency for pan frying.

While cooking the oatmeal in the stock, you should always use two to six bay leaves in the stock, to bring out that mild herby, piney flavor. The preferred oats are Dorsel's pinhead oats. Other varieties are Red Mill steel cut oats and McCann's Steel Cut Irish Oatmeal. You have to be wary of any product that claims to be steel cut but "fast cooking." The nature of steel cut oats, which are not rolled and processed like our morning oatmeal, is that they take longer to cook. Anyone who's used regular rolled oats in goetta knows that the end result is very mushy and crumbly, creating more of a "goetta mush" than with what we are most familiar. Pinhead oats give the right crunch, toothsomeness and mouth feel of goetta.

Salt and pepper should always be used to individual tastes. The rest of the spices can vary all over the map. My family's recipes have always called for only ground allspice. Some recipes will throw in several whole allspice berries during the cooking instead of the concentrated ground allspice. The Dorsel recipe calls for summer savory to replace onions, and some recipes show up with thyme, sage or marjoram, all of which are substitutes for summer savory. None of the older (at least three-generation) recipes call for garlic, which is not a common spice in the Cradle of Goetta. Also not in the earliest recipes is the use of ginger. Both are very aromatic and impart a strong flavor to the goetta. Hammann's Meats uses both of these aromatics in their goetta recipe, but its recipe comes from an Alsatian sausage maker. Other recent spice additions are red pepper and jalapeño for a spicier blend. If one wants a spicier goetta, I would recommend experimenting with paprika, a milder pepper than red pepper, or others. Some cooks will add poultry seasoning in the cooking liquid. The bottom line here is that the better cuts of meat you use, the more mild your spice choice should be—to taste, of course. If you use off cuts or organ meats like liver, then you might want to spice your goetta a bit stronger to offset the minerality of liver and organ meat. These goettas might include cinnamon, cloves, ginger or mace.

One large white onion should be used while cooking the meat. There is also a debate here as to how fine to chop the onion. Some like chunkier, some like more finely chopped. Our family recipe calls for the onion to be grated. After having tasted almost every goetta on the market, I'm somewhere in between the chunky vs. fine chopped options. Some recipes use one packet of Lipton's onion soup mix to replace onions. In my opinion, there's nothing better than the real thing—fresh onions. I have seen a few recipes that call for one or two celery ribs during the cooking of the meat, along with the onion. I would be interested to taste these types of goetta to see how strong the celeriac flavor comes through.

The meat should be cooked first and its juices added to cook the oatmeal. Once the meat and oatmeal are both cooked, the ground meat should be added and the pot stirred vigorously to incorporate the meat and oatmeal evenly. Once that's done, it should be cooked a short while, until a thick porridge-like consistency is achieved. If your cooked goetta is too thin and soupy, it will never congeal, so it needs to be the right consistency before being cooled in pans. When the right consistency is achieved, the goetta is poured into bread loaf pans and allowed to cook and congeal. Once congealed, it is sliced and panfried crispy or mushy depending on tastes and served with a variety of dressings and sides.

Then there comes the question of how to dress goetta. Some argue that it should be eaten plain and crispy. There is certainly a sweet vs. savory debate here. I come from a savory family that uses ketchup. There are others who prefer spicy mustard, like Handelmaier's, mayonnaise, salsa, green tomato relish or even Frisch's tartar sauce. Some even prefer hot sauce like Frank's. But there are also those who like the sweet side, with items like maple syrup, Karo syrup, molasses, treacle, honey or even fruit jams like strawberry, grape, blackberry or apricot. Some even dress it with applesauce or hot fried apples.

To be exotic, I've tried South African Peri-Peri sauce, sweet Thai chili sauce, Jamaican Pickapeppa Hot Mango Sauce and British brown sauce on goetta. British brown sauce is a lot like A1 Sauce, which is not for me, but the first three are really good dressings. Peri-Peri is spicy but not over the top. The mango sauce is a sweet and spicy sauce, offering the best of both worlds, as is the Thai chili sauce.

Next comes the question of what to serve with goetta. Over in Germany, grain sausages are served plain, undressed, with an acid, like fried apples, pears, sour pumpkin, kraut, pickles or pickled beetroot, and a starch, like fried potatoes, turnips or a bread. In Cincinnati, most serve it with eggs over easy with toast. The delight of dipping a bite in a runny warm yolk to many is best. Some like to serve it with eggs and breakfast potatoes or hash browns. Most restaurants in town have it as a choice of breakfast sausage along with bacon, a sausage patty or a sausage link on an egg plate. Others will even make a breakfast sandwich with the addition of a slice of cheese. A popular breakfast variation that is served at many restaurants in Cincinnati is Goetta Benedict, where it takes the place of Canadian bacon and is served over an English muffin or biscuit with a poached egg drenched in creamy hollandaise sauce.

One of the most creative ways to serve goetta with eggs comes from my buddy Scott P. He takes goetta and presses it into a pie pan and blind bakes it to be the crust of a quiche. Now that's goetta innovation. Perhaps the highest-cholesterol way of eating goetta I've heard of is fried with a slice of braunschwieger on white toast with ketchup. To each their own, but be sure to have your Lipitor handy.

Goetta will continue to evolve as both tastes and cooking products evolve. There are microwaveable products on the market. It has been incorporated into nearly every non-Germanic dish known, from egg rolls to pizza. We have certainly cemented goetta into our regional foodway for centuries to come. But I want to thank those humble Germanic immigrants, tired, hungry and of limited means, who came to our country seeking refuge and a better life and gave us this delicious porcine delight!

SELECTED BIBLIOGRAPHY

Interviews

Balasa, Mark. Personal interview, June 15, 2018.

Dorsel, Tom. Email correspondance, July 9, 2019.

Finke, Billy. Personal interview, April, 28, 2018.

Finke, Jeffery. Personal interview, July 10, 2018

Finke, Jim. Personal interview, April 28, 2018.

Glier, Dan. Personal interview, September, 19, 2014.

Hensler, Elmer. Personal interview, June 15, 2018.

Kluener, Jim. Personal interview, July 18, 2018.

Langen, Greg. Personal interview, July 14, 2018.

Stehlin, Dick. Personal interview, June 30, 2018.

Swain, Gary, Richardson Mills. Phone interview, August 8, 2018.

Books

Cincinnati Germania Society. *Germania Society Cookbook: Guten Appetit!* Waverly, IA: G & R Publishing, 2018.

Davidis, Henriette. *Praktisches Kochbuch fur die Deutschen in Amerika*. Milwaukee, WI: George Brumders Printing, 1897.

Glier's Goetta Recipe Book: A Guide to Gliers Goetta. Covington, KY: Gliers Meats Inc., 2006.

Jaqua, John. *Spengler's*. Napoleon, OH: self-published, 1992.

Kahn's American Beauty Meat Recipes. Cincinnati, OH: E. Kahn's Sons Co., 1932.

Minster Historical Society. *Minster's Heart and Heritage Cookbook*. Fletcher, OH: Friends and Family Cookbook Publishers, 2010.

Spector, Robert. *The Mom and Pop Store: True Stories from the Heart of America*. New York: Walker & Company, 2009.

Tolzmann, Don Heinrich. *German Cincinnati*. Charleston, SC: Arcadia Publishing, 2005.

Weaver, William Woys. *Country Scrapple: An American Tradition*. Mechanicsburg, PA: Stackpole Books, 2003.

Magazines and Newspapers

Bashor, Melissa W. "In Cleveland County, Livermush is King." *Our State Magazine*. February 23, 2015.

Batesville Herald Tribune. "Goetta Anyone?." March 14, 2006.

Cincinnati Enquirer. "Mystery Meats." May 4, 1987, 67.

Cincinnati Post & Times Star. "They've Canned Goetta and Jarred Frosting." December 9, 1954.

———. "Did You Ever See a Winking Cow." July 17, 1967, 11.

Drilling, Joanne. "Goetta Smackdown." *Cincinnati Magazine*, July 2015.

Gollmer, Richard. "Zur Geschicte der Wurst." *Cincinnatier Volksblatt*, January 25, 1918, 6.

Grain Dealer Journal 49, no. 1, Chicago, Illinois, July 10, 1922, American Association of Advertising Agencies.

The Operative Miller 24, no. 1 (January 1919): 279, Chicago, Illinois.

Poeth, Greg, "Gotta Get it to Get a Goetta," *Kentucky Post*, November 15, 1982.

Raver, Howard, "Talk About Goetta you Getta Finke," *Kentucky Post*, February 28, 1957.

Toledo Blade. "Geoff Burns, Spengler's Restaurant in Napoleon Celebrating 125 Years." August 13, 2017.

Western Hills Press. "Wasslers Continue 120 Year Old Business." January 14, 2015, A1, A2.

Other Resources

Memoirs of the Dorsel Family, John H. Dorsel, 1933.

INDEX

ABOUT THE AUTHOR

Dann Woellert has a passion for regional food history. He has explored many of the local delicacies of his beloved Cincinnati, treating the discovery process like food genealogy. While Dann has worked as a product marketer for over a decade, he is a true history geek and a student of his German heritage. He is associated with the Cincinnati Preservation Association, the German American Citizens League, several local historical societies and speaks throughout the region to organizations about food history. He is a five-time recipient of the Ohioana Award for Literary and Artistic Achievement. With the belief that food connects us all and is the best mode of diplomacy, he curates the food blog "Dann Woellert the Food Etymologist." His idea of the best goetta breakfast is one square slice of his mother's homemade goetta, fried crispy, dressed with ketchup, two eggs fried over easy and two buttered, toasted slices of salt rising bread.

Visit us at
www.historypress.com